Congressional
Research Service
Informing the legislative debate since 1914 _____

Agriculture and Related Agencies: FY2015 Appropriations

Jim Monke, Coordinator
Specialist in Agricultural Policy

July 30, 2014

Congressional Research Service

7-5700

www.crs.gov

R43669

Summary

The annual Agriculture appropriations bill provides funding for all of the U.S. Department of Agriculture (USDA) except the Forest Service. It also includes the Food and Drug Administration (FDA) and—in the House bill and in enacted bills in even-numbered fiscal years—the Commodity Futures Trading Commission (CFTC).

For FY2015, both the House and Senate Appropriations Committees reported their Agriculture appropriations bills (H.R. 4800 and S. 2389) in May 2014—the earliest joint action in years. The House considered H.R. 4800 on the floor on June 11, procedurally read through most of the bill, and adopted several amendments. The bill was left unfinished when floor action was suspended due to House Whip leadership changes and concern over expected amendments. The Senate began consideration of a minibus appropriation of three bills on June 19, of which Agriculture was Division C of a Senate amendment to H.R. 4660. But Senate consideration quickly stopped over a disagreement about procedures for amendments. Thus both bills remain unfinished at the chamber level, although each was considered for a time on the respective chamber floor.

The discretionary target for the FY2015 Agriculture appropriations bill in the House is $20.880 billion (the "302(b) allocation"), the same as for FY2014. The Senate's allocation is $20.575 billion, lower than the House bill in part due to the absence of CFTC in the Senate's jurisdiction.

In terms of budget amounts, both the House- and Senate-reported bills generally make small discretionary changes compared with FY2014. The Senate bill includes $143 million of emergency conservation and forestry spending, of which $100 million is offset by a disaster declaration that does not count against the discretionary spending limit. If the House and Senate bills are made comparable by excluding CFTC from the House bill, the Senate bill spends $13 million more than the House bill if the disaster designation is *not* counted, but officially is $87 million less than the House bill total *with* the disaster designation.

The Agricultural Research Service would receive $155 million more than FY2014 (+13%) in the House bill to fund requested construction. The Special Supplemental Nutrition Program for Women, Infants, and Children (WIC) is reduced by $92 million in both the House and Senate bills. Most other agencies receive small increases over FY2014 in both bills that are facilitated by higher offsets than in FY2014 in "scorekeeping adjustments" from better than expected results in appropriated loan programs, and continued offsets from changes in mandatory spending programs (CHIMPS). Both bills make an administrative change to shift the cost of rental expenses for facilities into agency budgets, rather than being paid out of a central account.

Mandatory spending in the reported bills totals $121.6 billion, which is $3 billion less than FY2014 mostly due to less farm program spending following the 2014 farm bill. Mandatory spending on child nutrition programs increases by $1.2 billion (+6%) and Supplemental Nutrition Assistance Program (SNAP) appropriations remain nearly constant at about $82.2 billion.

Notable policy riders affecting the Agriculture appropriation bill this year include limitations on implementing nutrition standards for the school meals programs (particularly a waiver in the House-reported bill) and provisions in both bills to prevent USDA from excluding white potatoes from the WIC program. Also, the House bill would restrict USDA from implementing some rules about livestock and poultry marketing practices and some country-of-origin labeling regulations. Both bills continue a provision to prevent federal inspection of horse slaughter facilities, and a House floor amendment was adopted for local and regional international food aid purchases.

Contents

Figures

Tables

Appendixes

Contacts

Scope of the Agriculture Appropriations Bill

The Agriculture appropriations bill—formally known as the Agriculture, Rural Development, Food and Drug Administration, and Related Agencies Appropriations Act—provides funding for:

- all of the U.S. Department of Agriculture (USDA) except the Forest Service, which is funded in the Interior appropriations bill,

- the Food and Drug Administration (FDA) in the Department of Health and Human Services, and

- in the House, the Commodity Futures Trading Commission (CFTC). In the Senate, the Financial Services bill contains CFTC appropriations. In even-numbered fiscal years, CFTC appears in the enacted Agriculture appropriation.

Jurisdiction is with the House and Senate Committees on Appropriations, and each Subcommittee on Agriculture, Rural Development, Food and Drug Administration, and Related Agencies. The bill includes both mandatory and discretionary spending, although most appropriations decision-making concerns the latter. **Figure 1** illustrates the distribution of agriculture appropriations spending among major divisions and agencies in the FY2014 appropriation.

Figure 1. FY2014 Agriculture and Related Agencies Appropriations

(budget authority in billions of dollars)

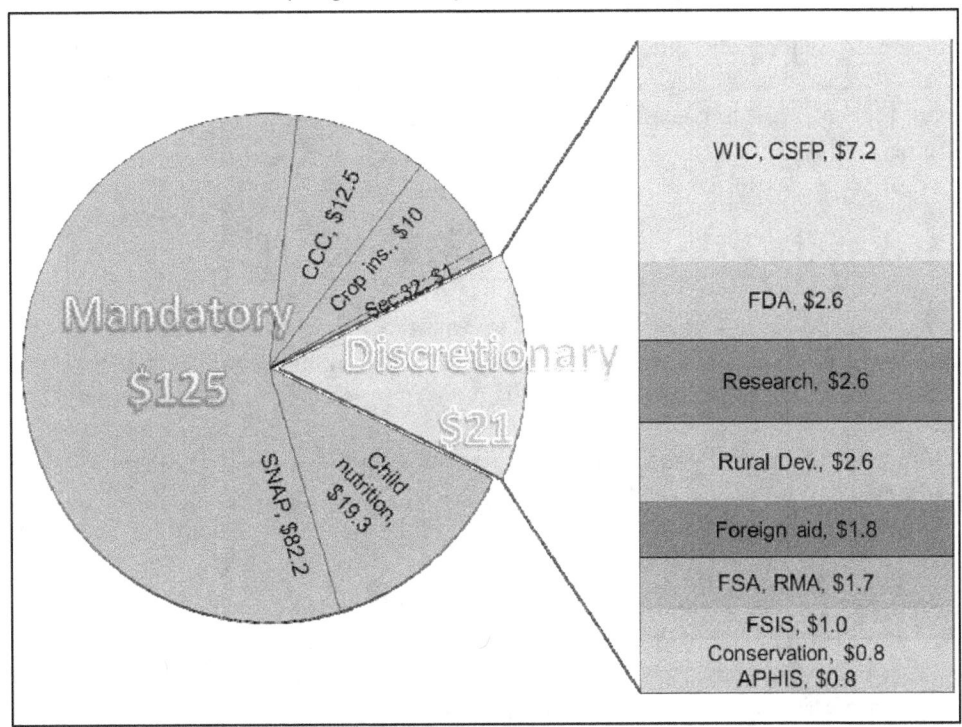

Source: CRS, compiled from P.L. 113-76. Does not show some agencies under $0.5 billion, including CFTC, AMS, GIPSA, and department administration that together are essentially offset by other reductions.

Note: CCC = Commodity Credit Corp.; SNAP = Supplemental Nutrition Assistance Program; WIC = Special Supplemental Nutrition Program for Women, Infants, and Children; CSFP = Commodity Supplemental Food Program; FDA = Food and Drug Admin.; FSA = Farm Service Agency; RMA = Risk Management Agency; FSIS = Food Safety Inspection Service; APHIS = Animal and Plant Health Inspection Service.

The federal budget process treats discretionary and mandatory spending differently.

- Discretionary spending is controlled by annual appropriations acts and consumes most of the attention during the appropriations process. The annual budget resolution process sets spending limits for discretionary appropriations. Agency operations (salaries and expenses) and many grant programs are discretionary.

- Mandatory spending—though carried in the appropriation and usually advanced unchanged—is controlled by budget enforcement rules (e.g., PAYGO) during the authorization process.[1] Spending for eligibility and benefit formulas in so-called entitlement programs are set in laws such as the farm bill and child nutrition act.[2]

In FY2014, about 14% ($20.9 billion) of the Agriculture appropriations bill—P.L. 113-76—was for discretionary programs. Mandatory spending carried in the bill totaled $124.6 billion, about 86% of the $145.2 billion total.

Within the discretionary total, the largest discretionary spending items are for the Special Supplemental Nutrition Program for Women, Infants, and Children (WIC), FDA, agricultural research, rural development, foreign food aid and trade, farm assistance program salaries and loans, food safety inspection, conservation, and animal and plant health programs (**Figure 1**).

The main mandatory spending items are the Supplemental Nutrition Assistance Program (SNAP, and other food and nutrition act programs), child nutrition (school lunch and related programs), crop insurance, and farm commodity and conservation programs paid through USDA's Commodity Credit Corporation (CCC).[3] SNAP is referred to as an "appropriated entitlement," and requires an annual appropriation.[4] The nutrition program amounts are based on projected spending needs. In contrast, the Commodity Credit Corporation operates on a line of credit with the Treasury; the annual appropriation provides funding to reimburse the Treasury for using the line of credit.

Action on FY2015 Appropriations[5]

Both the House and Senate Committees on Appropriations have reported their respective FY2015 Agriculture appropriations bills.[6] In each chamber, floor action has begun. But in both the House and Senate, proceedings stopped before the bills were completed or brought to a final vote.

Table 1 summarizes actions by the subcommittees, full committees and chambers, and enactment of each of the Agriculture appropriations bills since FY1995. Additional details for FY2015 are available for bill numbers and votes. **Figure 2** is a visual timeline of the dates in **Table 1**.

---

[1] CRS Report 98-560, *Baselines and Scorekeeping in the Federal Budget Process*.

[2] CRS Report R42484, *Budget Issues That Shaped the 2014 Farm Bill*.

[3] Mandatory spending in agriculture historically was reserved for programs such as the farm commodity programs and crop insurance that had uncertain outlays because of weather and market conditions. Mandatory spending creates funding stability and consistency compared to appropriations.

[4] CRS Report RS20129, *Entitlements and Appropriated Entitlements in the Federal Budget Process*.

[5] For a two-page summary of action and amounts in the House and Senate bills, see CRS Report IF00023, *FY2015 Agriculture and Related Agencies Appropriations (In Focus)*.

[6] See CRS Report R42388, *The Congressional Appropriations Process: An Introduction*, for context on procedures.

Table 1. Congressional Action on Agriculture Appropriations

Fiscal Year	House Action			Senate Action			Final Appropriation			CRS Report
	Subcom.	Comm.	Chamber	Subcom.	Comm.	Chamber	Enacted		Public Law[a]	
1995	5/26/1994	6/9/1994	6/17/1994	6/22/1994	6/23/1994	7/20/1994	9/30/1994	E	P.L. 103-330	IB94011
1996	6/14/1995	6/27/1995	7/21/1995	9/13/1995	9/14/1995	9/20/1995	10/21/1995	E	P.L. 104-37	95-624
1997	5/30/1996	6/6/1996	6/12/1996	7/10/1996	7/11/1996	7/24/1996	8/6/1996	E	P.L. 104-180	IB96015
1998	6/25/1997	7/14/1997	7/24/1997	7/15/1997	7/17/1997	7/24/1997	11/18/1997	E	P.L. 105-86	97-201
1999	6/10/1998	6/16/1998	6/24/1998	6/9/1998	6/11/1998	7/16/1998	10/21/1998	O	P.L. 105-277	98-201
2000	5/13/1999	5/24/1999	6/8/1999	6/15/1999	6/17/1999	8/4/1999	10/22/1999	E	P.L. 106-78	RL30201
2001	5/4/2000	5/16/2000	7/11/2000	5/4/2000	5/10/2000	7/20/2000	10/28/2000	E	P.L. 106-387	RL30501
2002	6/6/2001	6/27/2001	7/11/2001	Polled out	7/18/2001	10/25/2001	11/28/2001	E	P.L. 107-76	RL31001
2003	6/26/2002	7/26/2002	—	7/23/2002	7/25/2002	—	2/20/2003	O	P.L. 108-7	RL31301
2004	6/17/2003	7/9/2003	7/14/2003	7/17/2003	11/6/2003	11/6/2003	1/23/2004	O	P.L. 108-199	RL31801
2005	6/14/2004	7/7/2004	7/13/2004	9/8/2004	9/14/2004	—	12/8/2004	O	P.L. 108-447	RL32301
2006	5/16/2005	6/2/2005	6/8/2005	6/21/2005	6/27/2005	9/22/2005	11/10/2005	E	P.L. 109-97	RL32904
2007	5/3/2006	5/9/2006	5/23/2006	6/20/2006	6/22/2006	—	2/15/2007	Y	P.L. 110-5	RL33412
2008	7/12/2007	7/19/2007	8/2/2007	7/17/2007	7/19/2007	—	12/26/2007	O	P.L. 110-161	RL34132
2009	6/19/2008	—	—	Polled out	7/17/2008	—	3/11/2009	O	P.L. 111-8	R40000
2010	6/11/2009	6/18/2009	7/9/2009	Polled out	7/7/2009	8/4/2009	10/21/2009	E	P.L. 111-80	R40721
2011	6/30/2010	—	—	Polled out	7/15/2010	—	4/15/2011	Y	P.L. 112-10	R41475
2012	5/24/2011	5/31/2011	6/16/2011	Polled out	9/7/2011	11/1/2011	11/18/2011	O	P.L. 112-55	R41964
2013	6/6/2012	6/19/2012	—	Polled out	4/26/2012	—	3/26/2013	O	P.L. 113-6	R43110
2014	6/5/2013	6/13/2013	—	6/18/2013	6/20/2013	—	1/17/2014	O	P.L. 113-76	R43110
2015	5/20/2014 Draft[b] Voice vote	5/29/2013 H.R. 4800 H.Rept. 113-468 Vote of 31-18	tbd considered but unfinished 6/11/2014 H.R. 4800	5/20/2014 Voice vote	5/22/2014 S. 2389 S.Rept. 113-164 Vote 30-0c	tbd considered but unfinished 6/19/2014 H.R. 4660 Division C[d]	tbd		tbd	

Source: CRS.

a. E=Enacted as stand-alone appropriation; O=Omnibus appropriation; Y=Year-long continuing resolution.

b. The House subcommittee posted a draft of the bill at http://appropriations.house.gov/uploadedfiles/bills-113hr-sc-ap-fy2015-agriculture-subcommitteedraft.pdf. Amendments adopted in the full committee markup were posted at http://appropriations.house.gov/uploadedfiles/hmkp-113-ap00-20140529-sd005.pdf.

c. En bloc vote with the Military Construction-Veterans Affairs bill.

d. The Senate vehicle for floor consideration was "minibus" appropriation that included three committee-reported bills: Commerce-Justice-Science (Division A), Transportation-HUD (Division B), and Agriculture (Division C, of S.Amdt. 3244 to H.R. 4660).

Figure 2. Congressional Action on Agriculture Appropriations, FY1995-FY2015

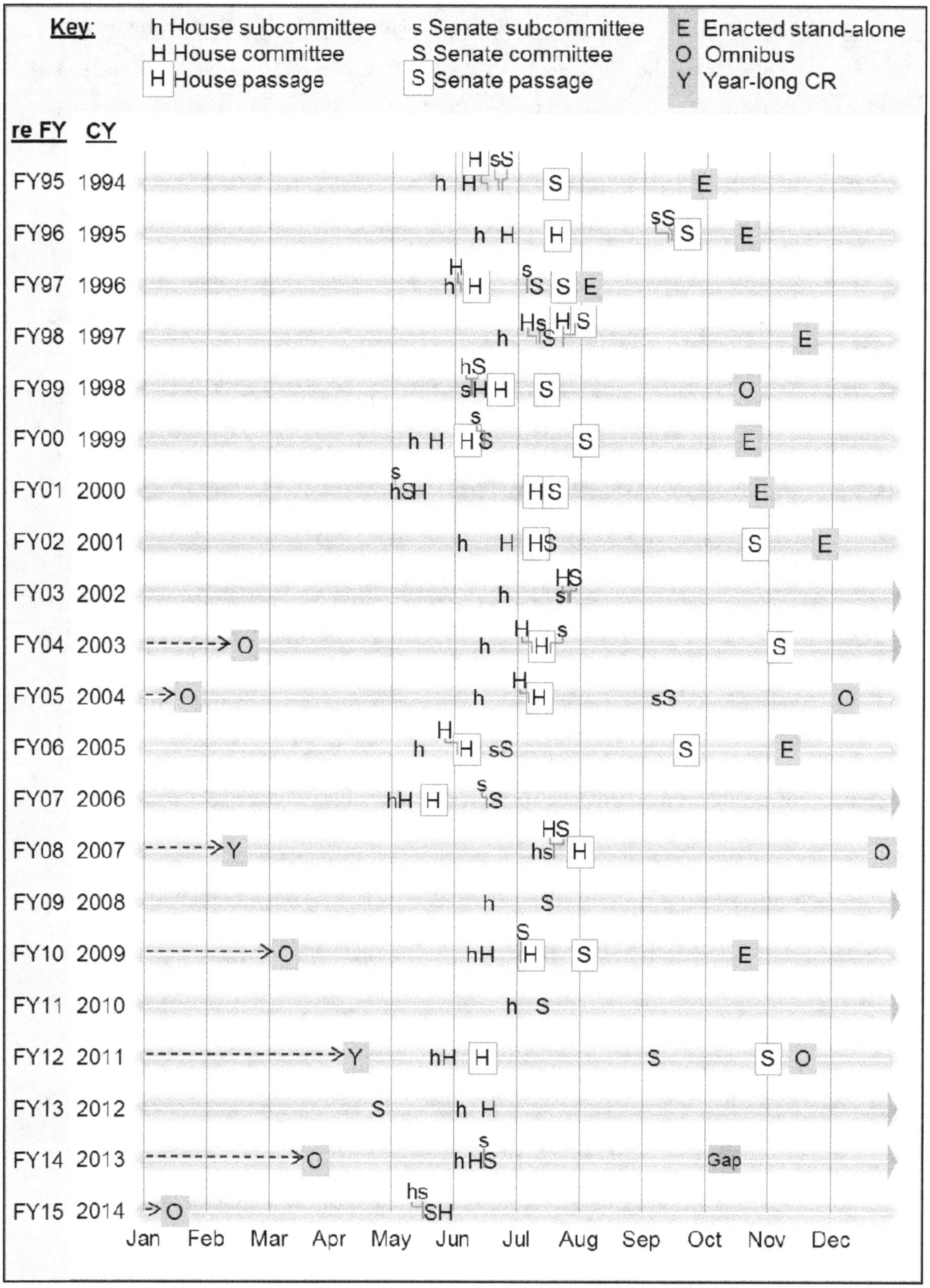

Source: CRS. Arrows indicate action was completed in a new calendar year. "Gap" is government shutdown.

Administration Budget Request

The Administration released its FY2015 budget request on March 4, 2014.[7] The Department of Agriculture concurrently released its budget summary[8] and detailed agency budget justifications.[9]

House Action

The Agriculture Subcommittee of the House Appropriations Committee held ten hearings on FY2015 appropriations with various USDA agencies, FDA, and CFTC from March 5, 2014, through April 8, 2014.

The subcommittee approved its FY2015 appropriations markup by voice vote on May 20, 2013.[10] The full House Appropriations Committee reported the bill (H.R. 4800; H.Rept. 113-468) on May 29, 2014, by a vote of 31-18 and officially reported it on June 4 (**Table 1**).

The rule for House floor consideration (H.Res. 616) was adopted on June 11, 2014, and House floor debate began later that day. Proceedings followed a modified open rule, with amendments debated under the five-minute rule (10 minutes of debate equally divided). H.R. 4800 was read through the end of Title VI (FDA and CFTC) and several amendments were adopted. However, the bill was left unfinished due to political changes in House Whip leadership and concern over expected amendments.[11] House appropriations action proceeded to other bills.

Senate Action

The Agriculture Subcommittee of the Senate Appropriations Committee held two hearings on the FY2015 appropriation—March 26, 2014, on the USDA budget request, and April 3, 2014, on the FDA budget request.

The subcommittee approved its FY2015 bill on May 20, 2014, by voice vote (**Table 1**). The full committee reported the bill (S. 2389, S.Rept. 113-164) on May 22 by a 30-0 vote.[12]

The Senate adopted cloture on June 17, 2014, to bring a three-bill "minibus" appropriation to the floor. The Agriculture portion was Division C of the minibus that included the Commerce-Justice-Science, Transportation-HUD, and Agriculture bills (S.Amdt. 3244 to H.R. 4660). However, proceedings stopped over disagreements about procedures for amendments, and by late July appropriations efforts had shifted to supplemental funding and a continuing resolution.[13]

---

[7] Office of Management and Budget (OMB), *Budget of the United States Government, Fiscal Year 2015*, at http://www.whitehouse.gov/omb/budget.

[8] USDA, *FY2015 Budget Summary,* April 2014, at http://www.obpa.usda.gov/budsum/FY15budsum.pdf.

[9] USDA, *FY2015 USDA Budget Explanatory Notes for Committee on Appropriations,* at http://www.obpa.usda.gov/FY15explan_notes.html.

[10] House subcommittee draft, http://appropriations.house.gov/uploadedfiles/bills-113hr-sc-ap-fy2015-agriculture-subcommitteedraft.pdf.

[11] Congressional Quarterly, "House Leadership Turmoil Latest Obstacle for Spending Bills," June 12, 2014.

[12] The 30-0 vote was an en bloc vote on the Military Construction-Veterans Affairs bill and the Agriculture bill.

[13] Congressional Quarterly, "With Senate Action Stalled, Continuing Resolution Looks Likely for Fall," July 18, 2014.

Legislative Action Compared With Prior Fiscal Years

This year's committee action on the FY2015 Agriculture appropriations bill is among the earliest in the last 20 years. Only for FY2001 did both chambers' committees complete action sooner. The delay in completing floor action in one or both chambers is more typical in recent years, though not with floor action occurring and being left unfinished.

The last time an Agriculture appropriations bill was enacted as a stand-alone measure was for FY2010 (in 2009). Floor action on an Agriculture appropriations bill has not occurred in the House or Senate since the FY2012 bill (in 2011).

In the 20 years since FY1995, Agriculture appropriations bills were enacted as stand-alone measures nine times. Omnibus appropriations were used nine times, and year-long continuing resolutions were used twice (**Table 1**; see also CRS Report RL32473, *Omnibus Appropriations Acts: Overview of Recent Practices.*)

At the subcommittee level, the Agriculture appropriations subcommittees in both the House and Senate have approved draft bills every year in this time period. The full appropriations committees usually report an Agriculture appropriations bill once one is passed by the subcommittee. The House Appropriations committee has reported an Agriculture appropriations bill every year except for FY2009 and FY2011. The Senate Appropriations committee has reported an Agriculture appropriations bill every year during this analysis.

Floor action in each chamber is somewhat less predictable, with House floor action not taking place for appropriations years FY2003, FY2009, FY2011, FY2013, and FY2014. In the Senate, floor action did not occur during those same five years, and also not for FY2005, FY2007, and FY2008 (when the House did pass bills).

In addition to the dates and appropriations acts for prior years, **Table 1** also lists the CRS report for each fiscal year.

Summary of Amounts in the Appropriation[14]

The Bipartisan Budget Act (P.L. 113-67, Dec. 26, 2013), set the total government-wide discretionary spending limits for both FY2014 and FY2015. These limits represented upward revisions of amounts that were originally targeted in the Budget Control Act of 2011 (P.L. 112-25). Total FY2015 discretionary spending is capped at $1.014 trillion (the "302(a) allocation").

An important congressional intention was to avoid budget sequestration on discretionary accounts in FY2014 and FY2015.[15] However, budget sequestration on non-exempt mandatory accounts does continue in these fiscal years (see "Sequestration of Mandatory Accounts" below).

Floor Action Began but Remains Unfinished

Although floor consideration has begun in each chamber and money-related amendments have been adopted on the House floor, neither bill has been adopted at the chamber level. None of the amendments approved on the floor have been included in the totals. Accordingly, this report presents the committee-reported amounts, since they are the most recent, comprehensive, and official amounts.

The enactment of the Bipartisan Budget Act substituted for the usual budget resolution process during the spring of 2014, and paved the way for action on FY2015 appropriations bills.[16]

---

[14] For a two-page summary of action and amounts in the House and Senate bills, see CRS Report IF00023, *FY2015 Agriculture and Related Agencies Appropriations (In Focus).*

[15] OMB, *Final Sequestration Report to the President and Congress for Fiscal Year 2014,* Feb. 7, 2014, at http://www.whitehouse.gov/sites/default/files/omb/assets/legislative_reports/sequestration/sequestration_final_feb2014.pdf.

[16] CRS Report R43535, *Provisions in the Bipartisan Budget Act of 2013 as an Alternative to a Traditional Budget Resolution.*

302(b) Subcommittee Allocations

Of the $1.014 trillion total government-wide discretionary spending limit for FY2015, the House Appropriations committee set a $20.880 billion discretionary limit for the Agriculture Appropriations bill (H.Rept. 113-454; the "302(b) allocation"). The total amount for the House bill is equal to the enacted amount in FY2014. The Senate allocation for the agriculture bill is $20.575 billion (S.Rept. 113-163). It is lower than the House bill and the FY2014 enacted level by $305 million, in large part due to the absence of CFTC in the Senate bill's jurisdiction which was $215 million in FY2014.

Comparison of Amounts for FY2015

Table 2 summarizes the amounts in the House-reported and Senate-reported appropriations bills, and compares them to three prior years and the Administration's request. The table lists the major agencies or programs in the appropriation, and the subtotals for titles in the bill.

Although floor consideration has begun in each chamber, and amendments have been adopted on the House floor, this report presents only the committee-reported amounts since neither bill has been adopted at the chamber level.

The House-reported bill's discretionary total is nearly the same as it was for last year: $20.868 billion for FY2015 compared with $20.880 billion in FY2014.

The Senate-reported bill total is harder to compare because of CFTC jurisdiction and because of disaster designations. The total of the Senate-reported Agriculture appropriations bill is $20.563 billion ($102 million less than the comparable $20.665 billion total from FY2014 without CFTC). This appears to be $87 million less than a comparable House total, but includes $100 million of emergency appropriations that are offset by a disaster designation. Thus, the total budget authority in the Senate bill regardless of the disaster designation would spend $13 million more than the House bill (on a Senate-comparable basis without CFTC). Regardless, the Senate-reported total is within +/- 0.5% of the comparable FY2014 and House levels.

Key Budget Terms

Budget authority is the main output of an appropriations act or a law authorizing mandatory spending. It provides the legal basis for agencies to obligate funds. It expires at the end of the period and usually is available for one year unless specified otherwise (such as two-year or indefinite authority). Most amounts in this report are budget authority.

Obligations reflect agency activities such as employing personnel or entering contracts. The Antideficiency Act prohibits agencies from obligating more budget authority than is provided in law.

Outlays are payments (cash disbursements) that satisfy a valid obligation. Outlays may differ from budget authority or obligations because payments from an agency may not occur until services are fulfilled, goods delivered, or construction completed, even though an obligation occurred.

Program level represents the sum of the activities supported or undertaken by an agency. A program level may be higher than a budget authority if the program (1) receives **user fees** that can be used to pay for activities; (2) makes or guarantees **loans** that are leveraged on the expectation of repayment (more than $1 of loan authority for $1 of budget authority); or (3) receives **transfers** from other agencies.

Rescissions are adjustments that cancel or reduce budget authority after it has been enacted; they score savings.

CHIMPS (Changes in Mandatory Program Spending) are adjustments to mandatory budget authority. CHIMPS in appropriations usually reduce or limit spending by mandatory programs and score budgetary savings.

For more background, see CRS Report 98-405, *The Spending Pipeline: Stages of Federal Spending.*

The Administration's request was nearly $450 million less than the House-reported and Senate-reported bills, though that difference is overstated because of sequestration scoring differences discussed later in a text box in the section "Changes in Mandatory Program Spending (CHIMPS)."

Sequestration of Mandatory Accounts

Sequestration is a process of automatic, largely across-the-board reductions that permanently cancel mandatory and/or discretionary budget authority to enforce statutory budget goals. The current requirement for sequestration is in the Budget Control Act of 2011 (BCA; P.L. 112-25).[17]

Although the Bipartisan Budget Act of 2013 (P.L. 113-67) raised spending limits in the BCA to avoid sequestration of discretionary accounts in FY2014 and FY2015, it did not reduce sequestration on mandatory accounts. In fact, to pay for avoiding sequestration in the near term, it extended by two years (until FY2023) the duration for sequestration on mandatory programs.[18]

Since enactment of the BCA, the Office of Management and Budget (OMB) has ordered budget sequestration on non-exempt, non-defense accounts at the following rates:

- FY2013: 5.1% from mandatory accounts, and 5.0% from discretionary accounts[19]

- FY2014: 7.2% from mandatory accounts,[20] and

- FY2015: 7.3% to mandatory accounts.[21]

Some farm bill mandatory programs are exempt from sequestration. The nutrition programs and the Conservation Reserve Program are exempt, and some prior legal obligations in crop insurance and the farm commodity programs may be exempt as determined by OMB.[22] However, many mandatory farm bill programs are subject to sequestration. Indeed, the Congressional Budget Office (CBO) baseline that was used to write the 2014 farm bill was affected by sequestration.[23]

USDA has announced that sequestration reductions will be necessary for a variety of its mandatory programs in FY2014, but it has not said specifically how it will implement the reductions.[24] In 2013, USDA sequestered a subset of mandatory programs at a higher rate than the 5.1% reduction because some payments on other programs already had gone out.[25] In 2014 and 2015, earlier notice may expand the number of programs affected. Sequestration issues are affecting some amounts in the FY2015 appropriation as discussed in the sections "Mandatory Conservation Programs" and "Changes in Mandatory Program Spending (CHIMPS)."

---

[17] See CRS Report R42972, *Sequestration as a Budget Enforcement Process: Frequently Asked Questions.*

[18] CBO, *Bipartisan Budget Act of 2013,* December 11, 2013, at http://cbo.gov/publication/44964.

[19] OMB, *Report to the Congress on the Joint Committee Sequestration for FY2013*, March 1, 2013, at http://www.white house.gov/sites/default/files/omb/assets/legislative_reports/fy13ombjcsequestrationreport.pdf.

[20] OMB, *Report to the Congress on the Joint Committee Reductions for FY2014*, May 20, 2013, http://www.white house.gov/sites/default/files/omb/assets/legislative_reports/fy14_preview_and_joint_committee_reductions_reports_05202013.pdf.

[21] OMB, *Report to the Congress on the Joint Committee Reductions for FY2015*, March 10, 2014, at http://www.white house.gov/sites/default/files/omb/assets/legislative_reports/sequestration_order_report_march2014.pdf.

[22] See 2 U.S.C. 905 (g)(1)(A), and 2 U.S.C. 906 (j). See also CRS Report R42050, *Budget "Sequestration" and Selected Program Exemptions and Special Rules.*

[23] For more background, see CRS Report R42484, *Budget Issues That Shaped the 2014 Farm Bill.*

[24] USDA Farm Service Agency, "FSA Advises Producers to Anticipate Payment Reductions Due to Mandated Sequester," November 13, 2013, at http://www.fsa.usda.gov/FSA/newsReleases?area=newsroom&subject=landing&topic=ner&newstype=newsrel&type=detail&item=nr_20131115_rel_0192 html.

[25] Capital Press, "Sequester leads USDA to cut direct payments 8.5 percent," at http://www.capitalpress.com/content/jh-direct-payments-040313.

Table 2. Agriculture and Related Agencies Appropriations, by Agency and Program

(budget authority in millions of dollars)

Agency or Major Program	FY2012 P.L. 112-55	FY2013 P.L. 113-6 post-seq.	FY2014 P.L. 113-76	FY2015 Admin. Request	FY2015 House-reported	FY2015 Senate-reported	Change from FY2014 to House $	Change from FY2014 to House %	Change from House to Senate $	Change from House to Senate %
SUMMARY by TITLE										
I: Agricultural Programs	24,970.2	27,938.8	29,938.1	25,526.9	25,707.3	25,627.3	-4,230.8	-14.1%	-80.0	-0.3%
Mandatory (M)	18,293.5	21,582.7	23,149.1	18,857.3	18,855.8	18,857.8	-4,293.3	-18.5%	+2.0	+0.0%
Discretionary	6,676.7	6,356.2	6,789.0	6,669.6	6,851.5	6,769.5	+62.5	+0.9%	-82.0	-1.2%
II: Conservation Programs	844.0	781.2	825.8	815.7	869.0	850.2	+43.1	+5.2%	-18.8	-2.2%
III: Rural Development	2,405.2	2,279.9	2,569.7	2,385.9	2,590.8	2,606.9	+21.1	+0.8%	+16.1	+0.6%
IV: Domestic Food Programs	105,553.0	104,098.0	108,585.6	112,047.9	109,825.3	109,802.9	+1,239.7	+1.1%	-22.4	-0.0%
Mandatory (M)	98,551.9	97,171.9	101,432.9	104,723.4	102,722.9	102,723.0	+1,290.0	+1.3%	+0.1	+0.0%
Discretionary	7,001.1	6,926.1	7,152.7	7,324.5	7,102.3	7,079.9	-50.4	-0.7%	-22.4	-0.3%
V: Foreign Assistance	1,835.7	1,705.9	1,838.5	1,777.0	1,856.0	1,843.2	+17.5	+1.0%	-12.8	-0.7%
VI: Food and Drug Administration	2,505.8	2,386.0	2,560.7	2,584.2	2,582.9	2,597.3	+22.2	+0.9%	+14.5	+0.6%
Commodity Futures Trading Commission[a]	205.3	[194.0]	215.0	280.0	217.6	[280.0]	+2.6	+1.2%	+62.4	+28.7%
VII: General Provisions: CHIMPS & rescissions	-1,650.7	-918.4	-987.0	-1,021.0	-792.0	-817.0	+195.0	-19.8%	-25.0	+3.2%
General Provisions: Other appropriations	377.1	132.5	106.6	2.0	0.0	143.3	-106.6	-100.0%	+143.3	na
Scorekeeping adjustments[b]	-72.0	-129.0	-191.0	-398.0	-410.0	-410.0	-219.0	+114.7%	+0.0	+0.0%
Subtract disaster declaration in this bill	-367.0					-100.0				
Discretionary: Senate basis w/o CFTC	[19,556.0]	19,520.5	[20,665.0]	20,139.8	[20,650.4]	20,563.4	-14.6	-0.1%	-87.1	-0.4%
Discretionary: House basis w/ CFTC	19,761.3	[19,714.5]	20,880.0	20,419.8	20,868.0	[20,843.4]	-12.0	-0.1%	-24.6	-0.1%
Mandatory subtotal (M)	116,845.4	118,754.6	124,582.0	123,581.2	121,578.7	121,580.8	-3,003.2	-2.4%	2.0	+0.0%
Total: Senate basis, w/o CFTC	136,401.4	138,275.0	145,247.0	143,720.9	142,229.2	142,144.1	-3,017.8	-2.1%	-85.0	-0.1%

Agency or Major Program	FY2012 P.L. 112-55	FY2013 P.L. 113-6 post-seq.	FY2014 P.L. 113-76	FY2015 Admin. Request	FY2015 House-reported	FY2015 Senate-reported	Change from FY2014 to House $	Change from FY2014 to House %	Change from House to Senate $	Change from House to Senate %
Title I: Agricultural Programs										
Departmental Administration	507.6	531.3	526.1	380.9	360.1	379.6	-166.1	-31.6%	+19.5	+5.4%
Research, Education and Economics										
Agricultural Research Service	1,094.6	1,016.9	1,122.5	1,104.4	1,275.3	1,139.7	+152.8	+13.6%	-135.6	-10.6%
National Institute of Food & Agriculture	1,202.3	1,142.0	1,277.1	1,335.5	1,273.8	1,292.4	-3.3	-0.3%	+18.6	+1.5%
National Agricultural Statistics Service	158.6	166.6	161.2	179.0	169.4	178.2	+8.2	+5.1%	+8.8	+5.2%
Economic Research Service	77.7	71.4	78.1	83.4	85.8	85.4	+7.7	+9.9%	-0.4	-0.5%
Under Sec. Research, Education, Economics	0.8	0.8	0.9	0.9	0.9	0.9	+0.0	+0.6%	+0.0	+0.0%
Marketing and Regulatory Programs										
Animal & Plant Health Inspection Service	819.7	761.4	824.9	837.5	870.7	875.6	+45.8	+5.6%	+4.9	+0.6%
Agricultural Marketing Service	83.4	75.7	81.3	84.2	82.4	83.0	+1.1	+1.4%	+0.6	+0.7%
Section 32 (M)	1,080.0	1,049.6	1,107.0	1,122.0	1,122.0	1,122.0	+15.0	+1.4%	+0.0	+0.0%
Grain Inspection, Packers & Stockyards	37.8	37.3	40.3	44.0	43.7	44.0	+3.5	+8.6%	+0.3	+0.7%
Under Secretary, Marketing and Regulatory	0.8	0.8	0.9	0.9	0.9	0.9	+0.0	+0.6%	+0.0	+0.0%
Food Safety										
Food Safety & Inspection Service	1,004.4	977.3	1,010.7	1,001.4	1,005.2	1,022.8	-5.5	-0.5%	+17.6	+1.7%
Under Secretary, Food Safety	0.8	0.8	0.8	0.8	0.8	0.8	+0.0	+0.6%	+0.0	+0.0%
Farm and Commodity Programs										
Farm Service Agency[c]	1,612.5	1,503.9	1,592.2	1,539.4	1,605.1	1,589.1	+12.9	+0.8%	-16.0	-1.0%
FSA Farm Loans: Loan Authority[d]	4,787.1	4,575.7	5,527.3	6,402.1	6,402.1	6,402.1	+874.8	+15.8%	+0.0	+0.0%
Risk Management Agency Salaries & Exp.[e]	74.9	69.1	71.5	76.8	77.1	76.8	+5.6	+7.8%	-0.3	-0.4%
Federal Crop Insurance Corporation[e]	3,142.4	9,514.5	9,502.9	8,668.0	8,666.0	8,668.0	-836.9	-8.8%	+2.0	+0.0%
Commodity Credit Corporation[e]	14,071.0	11,018.5	12,538.9	9,067.3	9,067.3	9,067.3	-3,471.6	-27.7%	+0.0	+0.0%

Agency or Major Program	FY2012 P.L. 112-55	FY2013 P.L. 113-6 post-seq.	FY2014 P.L. 113-76	Admin. Request	FY2015 House-reported	FY2015 Senate-reported	Change from FY2014 to House $	Change from FY2014 to House %	Change from House to Senate $	Change from House to Senate %
Under Secretary, Farm and Foreign Agric.	0.8	0.8	0.9	0.9	0.9	0.9	+0.0	+0.6%	+0.0	+0.0%
Subtotal										
Mandatory (M)	18,293.5	21,582.7	23,149.1	18,857.3	18,855.8	18,857.8	-4,293.3	-18.5%	+2.0	+0.0%
Discretionary	6,676.7	6,356.2	6,789.0	6,669.6	6,851.5	6,769.5	+62.5	+0.9%	-82.0	-1.2%
Subtotal	24,970.2	27,938.8	29,938.1	25,526.9	25,707.3	25,627.3	-4,230.8	-14.1%	-80.0	-0.3%
Title II: Conservation Programs										
Conservation Operations	828.2	766.8	812.9	814.8	843.1	849.3	+30.1	+3.7%	+6.2	+0.7%
Watershed Rehabilitation Program	15.0	13.6	12.0	0.0	25.0	0.0	+13.0	+108.3%	-25.0	-100.0%
Under Secretary, Natural Resources	0.8	0.8	0.9	0.9	0.9	0.9	+0.0	+0.6%	+0.0	+0.0%
Subtotal	844.0	781.2	825.8	815.7	869.0	850.2	+43.1	+5.2%	-18.8	-2.2%
Title III: Rural Development										
Salaries and Expenses (including transfers)	653.9	613.0	657.4	659.6	678.2	682.9	+20.8	+3.2%	+4.7	+0.7%
Rural Housing Service	1,090.3	1,031.1	1,279.6	1,228.6	1,310.4	1,307.0	+30.7	+2.4%	-3.4	-0.3%
RHS Loan Authority^d	26,546.0	27,335.1	27,408.1	26,803.6	27,563.9	27,423.6	+155.8	+0.6%	-140.3	-0.5%
Rural Business-Cooperative Service^f	109.3	114.2	130.2	139.2	99.6	111.7	-30.6	-23.5%	+12.2	+12.3%
RBCS Loan Authority^d	869.8	953.7	1,022.8	772.5	1,028.7	1,022.8	+5.8	+0.6%	-5.8	-0.6%
Rural Utilities Service	551.0	520.8	501.6	357.6	501.8	504.4	+0.2	+0.0%	+2.6	+0.5%
RUS Loan Authority^d	8,676.9	8,849.4	7,514.5	6,589.2	7,498.8	7,474.4	-15.7	-0.2%	-24.4	-0.3%
Under Secretary, Rural Development	0.8	0.8	0.9	0.9	0.9	0.9	+0.0	+0.6%	+0.0	+0.0%
Subtotal^f	2,405.2	2,279.9	2,569.7	2,385.9	2,590.8	2,606.9	+21.1	+0.8%	+16.1	+0.6%
Subtotal, RD Loan Authority^d	36,092.7	37,138.2	35,945.4	34,165.3	36,091.3	35,920.8	+145.9	+0.4%	-170.5	-0.5%

Agency or Major Program	FY2012 P.L. 112-55	FY2013 P.L. 113-6 post-seq.	FY2014 P.L. 113-76	Admin. Request	FY2015 House-reported	FY2015 Senate-reported	Change from FY2014 to House $	%	Change from House to Senate $	%
Title IV: Domestic Food Programs										
Child Nutrition Programs (M)	18,151.2	19,913.2	19,288.0	20,537.0	20,523.8	20,497.0	+1,235.8	+6.4%	-26.8	-0.1%
WIC Program	6,618.5	6,522.2	6,715.8	6,823.0	6,623.0	6,623.0	-92.8	-1.4%	+0.0	+0.0%
SNAP, Food & Nutrition Act Programs (M)	80,401.7	77,285.4	82,169.9	84,256.4	82,251.1	82,251.4	+81.2	+0.1%	+0.2	+0.0%
Commodity Assistance Programs	242.3	243.7	269.7	275.7	275.7	275.7	+6.0	+2.2%	+0.0	+0.0%
Nutrition Programs Administration	138.5	132.7	141.3	155.0	150.8	155.0	+9.5	+6.7%	+4.2	+2.8%
Office of Under Secretary	0.8	0.8	0.8	0.8	0.8	0.8	+0.0	+0.6%	+0.0	+0.0%
Subtotal										
Mandatory (M)	**98,551.9**	**97,171.9**	**101,432.9**	**104,723.4**	**102,722.9**	**102,723.0**	**+1,290.0**	**+1.3%**	**+0.1**	**+0.0%**
Discretionary	**7,001.1**	**6,926.1**	**7,152.7**	**7,324.5**	**7,102.3**	**7,079.9**	**-50.4**	**-0.7%**	**-22.4**	**-0.3%**
Subtotal	**105,553.0**	**104,098.0**	**108,585.6**	**112,047.9**	**109,825.3**	**109,802.9**	**+1,239.7**	**+1.1%**	**-22.4**	**-0.0%**
Title V: Foreign Assistance										
Foreign Agricultural Service	176.3	163.1	177.9	182.6	182.6	182.8	+4.7	+2.6%	+0.2	+0.1%
Public Law (P.L.) 480	1,468.5	1,362.0	1,468.7	1,402.5	1,468.5	1,468.5	-0.2	-0.0%	+0.0	+0.0%
McGovern-Dole Food for Education	184.0	174.5	185.1	185.1	198.1	185.1	+13.0	+7.0%	-13.0	-6.6%
CCC Export Loan Salaries	6.8	6.3	6.7	6.7	6.7	6.7	+0.0	+0.0%	+0.0	+0.0%
Subtotal	**1,835.7**	**1,705.9**	**1,838.5**	**1,777.0**	**1,856.0**	**1,843.2**	**+17.5**	**+1.0%**	**-12.8**	**-0.7%**
Title VI: Related Agencies										
Food and Drug Administration	2,505.8	2,386.0	2,560.7	2,584.2	2,582.9	2,597.3	+22.2	+0.9%	+14.5	+0.6%
Commodity Futures Trading Commission	205.3	[194.0]	215.0	280.0	217.6	[280.0]	+2.6	+1.2%	+62.4	+28.7%
Subtotal	**2,711.1**	**2,386.0**	**2,775.7**	**2,864.2**	**2,800.4**	**2,597.3**	**+24.8**	**+0.9%**	na	na

Agency or Major Program	FY2012 P.L. 112-55	FY2013 P.L. 113-6 post-seq.	FY2014 P.L. 113-76	FY2015 Admin. Request	FY2015 House-reported	FY2015 Senate-reported	Change from FY2014 to House $	Change from FY2014 to House %	Change from House to Senate $	Change from House to Senate %
Title VII: General Provisions										
Changes in Mandatory Program Spending^f	-1,631.8	-893.0	-953.7	-1,008.0	-779.0	-804.0	+174.7	-18.3%	-25.0	+3.2%
Rescissions	-18.9	-25.3	-33.3	-13.0	-13.0	-13.0	+20.3	-61.0%	+0.0	+0.0%
Other appropriations	377.1	132.5	106.6	2.0	0.0	143.3	-106.6	-100.0%	+143.3	na
Subtotal	**-1,273.6**	**-785.9**	**-880.4**	**-1,019.0**	**-792.0**	**-673.7**	**+88.4**	**-10.0%**	**+118.3**	**-14.9%**
Scorekeeping Adjustments^b										
Disaster declaration in this bill	-367.0					-100.0			-100.0	na
Other scorekeeping adjustments	-72.0	-129.0	-191.0	-398.0	-410.0	-410.0	-219.0	+114.7%	+0.0	+0.0%
Subtotal	**-439.0**	**-129.0**	**-191.0**	**-398.0**	**-410.0**	**-510.0**	**-219.0**	**+114.7%**	**-100.0**	**+24.4**

Source: CRS, compiled from tables in the joint explanatory statements or committee reports for S. 2389, H.R. 4800, P.L. 113-76, and P.L. 112-55. Senate CFTC amount is subcommittee markup. FY2013 post-sequestration amounts are from the USDA FY2013 Operating Plan. Scorekeeping adjustments are from unpublished Congressional Budget Office (CBO) tables.

Notes: [Bracketed amounts] are not in the official totals due to differing House-Senate jurisdiction for CFTC, but are shown for comparison. Amounts are in nominal dollars, and are budget authority in millions of dollars. Amounts do not include supplemental appropriations outside the annual appropriation.

a. Jurisdiction for CFTC is in the House Agriculture Appropriations subcommittee and the Senate Financial Services Appropriations subcommittee. After FY2008, CFTC is carried in enacted Agriculture appropriations in even-numbered fiscal years, always in House Agriculture markup, and never in Senate Agriculture markup.

b. "Scorekeeping adjustments" are not necessarily appropriated items and may not be shown in appropriations committee tables, but are part of the official CBO score (accounting) of the bill. They predominately include "negative subsidies" in loan program accounts, and adjustments for disaster designations in the bill.

c. Includes regular FSA salaries and expenses, plus transfers for farm loan program salaries and expenses and farm loan program administrative expenses. Also includes farm loan program loan subsidy, State Mediation Grants; Dairy Indemnity Program (mandatory funding); and Grassroots Source Water Protection Program. Does not include amounts appropriated to the Foreign Agricultural Service for export loans and P.L. 480 administration and transferred to FSA.

d. Loan authority is the amount of loans that can be made or guaranteed with a loan subsidy; it is not added in the budget authority subtotals or totals.

e. Commodity Credit Corporation and Federal Crop Insurance Corporation each receive an indefinite appropriation ("such sums as necessary"). Estimates are used in the appropriations bill reports and may not reflect actual outlays or reimbursements.

f. Amounts for the Rural Business Cooperative Service are before the rescission from the Cushion of Credit account. This allows the RBS total to remain positive, unlike in Appropriations committee tables. The rescission is included with the changes in mandatory program spending (CHIMPS) in the General Provisions section.

USDA Agencies and Programs

About 95% of the total appropriation for the U.S. Department of Agriculture (USDA) is funded through the Agriculture appropriations bill. The Department was created in 1862 and carries out widely varied responsibilities through about 30 separate internal agencies and offices staffed by nearly 100,000 employees.[26] Funding for about two-thirds of those employees is provided in the Agriculture appropriation. The remaining one-third of the employees, about 33,000 staff years, are in the Forest Service, funded by the Interior and Related Agencies Appropriations bill.[27]

This report is organized in the order that the agencies are listed in the Agriculture appropriations bill (except for the portion of FDA appropriations for food safety, which is discussed in a comprehensive section on food safety). See **Table 2** and tables in some of the following sections for more details on the amounts for specific agencies.

USDA Compared to the Appropriations Bill

Agriculture appropriations are not perfectly correlated with USDA spending. Agriculture appropriations include the FDA and CFTC (that are outside USDA), and do not fund the Forest Service (that is part of USDA). The Forest Service is funded in the Interior and Related Agencies appropriations bill.

Similarly, USDA spending is not synonymous with farm program spending. It includes programs that may not be considered agricultural, such as nutrition assistance and rural development.

USDA divides its activities into **mission areas** that are different from how the appropriation is organized in titles.

- Food and nutrition programs—with more than three-fourths of USDA's budget—comprise USDA's largest mission area. This is Title IV of the appropriation.

- The second-largest mission area, with about one-eighth of USDA's budget, is farm and foreign agricultural services. This mission area is split between appropriations Title I (domestic) and Title V (foreign trade and aid).

- Five other mission areas share one-eighth of USDA's budget, including natural resources, rural development, research, marketing and regulatory programs, and food safety. In appropriations bills, rural development is Title III, and conservation is Title II (the part of the natural resources mission area without the Forest Service). The other three mission areas others are combined into Title I of the appropriation.

The type of funding (mandatory or discretionary) also is an important difference between how the appropriations bill and USDA's mission areas are organized.

- USDA mission area totals include both mandatory and discretionary spending.

- In the appropriation, conservation (Title II), rural development (Title III), and agricultural research (part of Title I) include only discretionary amounts. Mandatory amounts for these programs are contained within the Commodity Credit Corporation amount in Title I.

---

[26] USDA, *FY2015 Budget Summary*, April 2014, p. 112, at http://www.obpa.usda.gov/budsum/FY15budsum.pdf.

[27] See CRS Report R43142, *Interior, Environment, and Related Agencies: FY2013 and FY2014 Appropriations*.

Departmental Administration[28]

The Agriculture appropriations bill has several accounts that provide for the general administration of the USDA, ranging from the immediate Office of the Secretary, to the Office of Inspector General, to facilities rental payments.

One notable administrative change for FY2015 is that both the House- and Senate-reported bills alter the accounting for rental expenses. Although the federal government owns many of the facilities in which agencies are housed, USDA rents some buildings and facilities from private vendors. In the past, all of USDA's rental obligations ($178 million in FY2014) were paid from a separate account at the Department level. For FY2015, both the House and Senate concur with the Administration's request that such payments be paid by the individual agencies. Thus, despite savings at the Departmental Administration level, many agency budgets are increased to compensate for the additional obligations. If agencies' budgets are not increased by at least the amount of rental payments being shifted, their net appropriation may reflect an effective decrease from prior years. The effect of shifting these costs into agency budgets is noted for many agencies later in this report. Therefore, the more than $150 million proposed decreases in Departmental Administration is largely due to the accounting change in rental payments, and is offset by diffuse and corresponding increases in individual agency budgets.

For FY2015, the House-reported bill would provide $360 million for Departmental Administration (**Table 3**). Some of the increases for administrative agencies and offices over FY2014 are, in part, to pay for the addition of rental payments in their budgets.

The Senate-reported bill would provide $380 million for Departmental Administration, $20 million more than the House bill. The differences between the House and Senate bills are the that the Office of Communications, General Counsel, and Departmental Administration would receive the President's requested amount, rather than a smaller House-reported amount. The Senate bill also provides $10 million more than the House bill and FY2014 for building operations and maintenance, the level requested by the Administration.

---

[28] This section was written by Jim Monke (7-9664, jmonke@crs.loc.gov).

Table 3. USDA Departmental Administration Appropriations
(budget authority in millions of dollars)

Administrative Office	FY2012 P.L. 112-55	FY2013 P.L. 113-6 post-seq.	FY2014 P.L. 113-76	FY2015 Admin. Request	FY2015 House-reported	FY2015 Senate-reported	Change from FY2014 to House $	Change from FY2014 to House %	Change from House to Senate $	Change from House to Senate %
Office of the Secretary										
Office of the Secretary	4.55	4.69	5.05	5.09	5.05	5.09	+0.0	+0.0%	+0.0	+0.7%
Office of Tribal Relations	0.45	0.46	0.50	0.50	0.50	0.50	+0.0	+0.0%	+0.0	+0.8%
Office of Homeland Security	1.32	1.39	1.50	1.51	1.51	1.51	+0.0	+0.7%	+0.0	+0.0%
Advocacy and Outreach	1.21	1.32	1.21	1.22	1.21	1.22	+0.0	+0.0%	+0.0	+0.7%
Assistant Secretary for Admin.	0.76	0.75	0.80	0.81	0.80	0.81	+0.0	+0.0%	+0.0	+0.6%
Departmental Administration	24.17	22.50	22.79	25.66	22.81	25.31	+0.0	+0.1%	+2.5	+11.0%
Asst. Sec. Congressional Relations	3.58	3.59	3.87	3.90	3.87	3.90	+0.0	+0.0%	+0.0	+0.7%
Office of Communications	8.07	8.36	8.07	8.14	5.54	8.14	-2.5	-31.4%	+2.6	+47.0%
Subtotal, Office of the Secretary	**44.10**	**43.06**	**43.78**	**46.82**	**41.28**	**46.47**	**-2.5**	**-5.7%**	**+5.2**	**+12.6%**
Executive Operations										
Office of Chief Economist	11.18	15.01	16.78	16.85	16.78	16.85	+0.0	+0.0%	+0.1	+0.5%
National Appeals Division	12.84	13.19	12.84	13.43	13.32	13.43	+0.5	+3.7%	+0.1	+0.8%
Office of Budget, Program Analysis	8.95	8.35	9.06	10.29	9.39	9.31	+0.3	+3.6%	-0.1	-0.9%
Subtotal, Executive Operations	**32.96**	**36.56**	**38.68**	**40.58**	**39.49**	**39.59**	**+0.8**	**+2.1%**	**+0.1**	**+0.3%**
Other Administration										
Chief Information Officer	44.03	40.65	44.03	45.20	45.03	45.20	+1.0	+2.3%	+0.2	+0.4%
Chief Financial Officer	5.65	5.77	6.21	6.08	6.03	6.08	-0.2	-3.0%	+0.1	+0.9%
Assistant Secretary for Civil Rights	0.85	0.83	0.89	0.90	0.90	0.90	+0.0	+0.6%	+0.0	+0.0%
Office of Civil Rights	21.00	21.02	21.40	24.24	24.07	24.24	+2.7	+12.5%	+0.2	+0.7%

Administrative Office	FY2012 P.L. 112-55	FY2013 P.L. 113-6 post-seq.	FY2014 P.L. 113-76	FY2015 Admin. Request	FY2015 House-reported	FY2015 Senate-reported	Change from FY2014 to House $	Change from FY2014 to House %	Change from House to Senate $	Change from House to Senate %
Buildings, facilities, and rental payments	230.42	252.40	233.00	64.83	54.83	64.84	-178.2	-76.5%	+10.0	+18.3%
Hazardous materials management	3.59	3.70	3.59	3.60	3.60	3.60	+0.0	+0.2%	+0.0	+0.0%
Office of Inspector General	85.62	82.30	89.90	97.24	97.02	97.24	+7.1	+7.9%	+0.2	+0.2%
General Counsel	39.35	41.87	41.20	47.57	44.38	47.57	+3.2	+7.7%	+3.2	+7.2%
Office of Ethics	na	3.14	3.44	3.87	3.44	3.87	+0.0	+0.0%	+0.4	+12.4%
Subtotal, Other Administration	**430.50**	**451.68**	**443.67**	**293.51**	**279.29**	**293.53**	**-164.4**	**-37.1%**	**+14.2**	**+5.1%**
Total, Departmental Administration	**507.57**	**531.30**	**526.13**	**380.90**	**360.06**	**379.59**	**-166.1**	**-31.6%**	**+19.5**	**+5.4%**

Source: CRS, compiled from tables in the joint explanatory statements or committee reports for S. 2389, H.R. 4800, P.L. 113-76, and P.L. 112-55. Post-sequestration amounts for FY2013 are from the USDA FY2013 Operating Plan.

Agricultural Research, Education, and Extension[29]

Four agencies carry out USDA's research, education, and economics (REE) mission:

- The **Agricultural Research Service (ARS)**, USDA's intramural science agency, conducts long-term, high-risk, basic and applied research on food and agriculture issues of national and regional importance.

- The **National Institute of Food and Agriculture (NIFA)** distributes federal funds to land grant colleges of agriculture to provide partial support for state-level research, education, and extension.

- The **National Agricultural Statistics Service (NASS)** collects and publishes current national, state, and county agricultural statistics. NASS also is responsible for administration of the Census of Agriculture, which occurs every five years and provides comprehensive data on the U.S. agricultural economy.

- The **Economic Research Service (ERS)** provides economic analysis of issues regarding public and private interests in agriculture, natural resources, food, and rural America.

For FY2015, the House-reported bill would provide $2.804 billion to the USDA REE mission area ($165 million, or +6.3%, more than FY2014). The Senate bill would provide $2.696 billion ($109 million less than the House bill, but still an increase from FY2014 and consistent with the Administration's base request). After FY2010, none of the annual appropriations have included any earmarks or congressionally designated spending items for REE-related activities.

Across REE, most of the increase in the House-reported bill is for ARS buildings and facilities (+$155 million), though NASS and ERS receive larger proportional increases of +5% and +10%, respectively (**Table 4**). The Senate bill does not provide any funding for ARS buildings and facilities that the House proposes, but compared to the House-reported bill provides $19 million more to ARS salaries and expenses, $19 million more for NIFA, and $9 million more to NASS.

In addition to its base request, the Administration proposed an additional $277 million for ARS and NIFA under an Opportunity, Growth, and Security (OGS) Initiative.[30] With the exception of the buildings and facilities appropriation in the House-reported bill, neither the House nor Senate bill funds this initiative.

The increases in the FY2014 and FY2015 funding levels for REE activities come after three years of reductions. Appropriations to the REE mission area declined nearly 16% from FY2010 to FY2013. ARS appropriations declined nearly 19% and NIFA by 15% from FY2010 to FY2013. The increases for the mission area in FY2014 and FY2015 restore most of those reductions since FY2010 in absolute terms, if not inflation-adjusted terms. The amount for ARS in the House bill would exceed the FY2010 level ($1.25 billion), but neither bill yet achieves the FY2010 level for NIFA ($1.34 billion). Thus, agricultural research stakeholders continue to express concern for research funding over the long term.

---

[29] This section was written by Jim Monke (7-9664, jmonke@crs.loc.gov).

[30] For background, see CRS Report R43580, *Federal Research and Development Funding: FY2015.*

Table 4. USDA Research, Extension, and Economics (REE) Appropriations

(budget authority in millions of dollars)

Agency or Major Program	FY2012 P.L. 112-55	FY2013 P.L. 113-6 post-sequ.	FY2014 P.L. 113-76	FY2015 Admin. Request (base)	FY2015 Admin. OGS initiative	FY2015 House-reported	FY2015 Senate-reported	Change from FY2014 to House $	Change from FY2014 to House %	Change from House to Senate $	Change from House to Senate %
Agricultural Research Service	1,094.6	1,016.9	1,122.5	1,104.4	47.2	1,120.3	1,139.7	-2.2	-0.2%	+19.4	+1.7%
Buildings and Facilities	0.0	0.0	0.0	0.0	155.0	155.0	0.0	+155.0	na	-155.0	na
National Institute of Food & Agric.	1,202.3	1,142.0	1,277.1	1,335.5	80.0	1,273.8	1,292.4	-3.3	-0.3%	+18.6	+1.5%
Research and Education	705.6	683.2	772.6	837.7	80.0	774.5	787.5	+1.9	+0.2%	+13.1	+1.7%
AFRI (competitive grants)	264.5	275.6	316.4	325.0	60.0	325.0	325.0	+8.6	+2.7%	+0.0	+0.0%
Hatch Act (1862 institutions)	236.3	218.6	243.7	243.7	15.0	243.7	243.7	+0.0	+0.0%	+0.0	+0.0%
Evans-Allen (1890s institutions)	50.9	47.1	52.5	52.5	5.0	52.5	52.5	+0.0	+0.0%	+0.0	+0.0%
McIntire-Stennis (forestry)	32.9	30.5	34.0	34.0		34.0	34.0	+0.0	+0.0%	+0.0	+0.0%
Innovation Institutes				75.0		0.0	0.0				
Other	121.0	111.5	126.0	107.6		119.3	132.4	-6.7	-5.3%	+13.1	+11.0%
Extension	475.2	439.1	469.2	469.0		467.3	472.7	-1.9	-0.4%	+5.3	+1.1%
Smith-Lever (b) & (c)	294.0	271.3	300.0	300.0		300.0	300.0	+0.0	+0.0%	+0.0	+0.0%
Smith-Lever (d)	99.3	91.7	85.5	85.7		85.7	85.5	+0.2	+0.2%	-0.2	-0.2%
Other	81.8	76.1	83.7	83.2		81.6	87.2	-2.1	-2.5%	+5.5	+6.8%
Integrated Activities	21.5	19.8	35.3	28.8		32.0	32.2	-3.3	-9.4%	+0.2	+0.7%
National Agric. Statistics Service	158.6	166.6	161.2	179.0		169.4	178.2	+8.2	+5.1%	+8.8	+5.2%
Economic Research Service	77.7	71.4	78.1	83.4		85.8	85.4	+7.7	+9.9%	-0.4	-0.5%
Total REE appropriation	2,533.3	2,397.0	2,638.8	2,702.4	277.2	2,804.2	2,695.6	+165.4	+6.3%	-108.6	-3.9%

Source: CRS, compiled from tables in the joint explanatory statements or committee reports for S. 2389, H.R. 4800, P.L. 113-76, and P.L. 112-55. Post-sequestration amounts for FY2013 are from the USDA FY2013 Operating Plan.

Agricultural Research Service

For FY2015, the House-reported bill would provide $1.120 billion for ARS salaries and expenses and $155 million for ARS buildings and facilities construction. The House-reported amount for salaries and expenses is about even with the FY2014 amount, though it reflects an effective reduction of about $7 million from FY2014 after adjusting for the inclusion of building rental payments.

The $155 million for buildings and facilities construction in the House bill was requested by the Administration in the Opportunity, Growth, and Security (OGS) Initiative. It would construct a new bio-containment facility to replace the Poultry Research Facility in Athens, GA. There has been no appropriation for ARS buildings and facilities in recent years. The OGS Initiative is not included in the request column of Appropriations committee tables, but is shown in **Table 4**.

The Senate bill would provide $1.140 billion for salaries and expenses, about $19 million more than the House bill, and nothing for buildings and facilities construction. The Senate-reported amount is $17 million more than the FY2014 amount, which is about $12 million more after adjusting for the inclusion of rental payments.

Both the House and Senate report language reject the Administration's request to close six ARS research centers and to redirect research programs at other laboratories.

In addition to the base request for ARS and the OGS Initiative for buildings and facilities, the Administration proposed an additional $42 million in the Opportunity, Growth, and Security (OGS) Initiative to support five high-priority research areas across the agency. Neither the House nor Senate bill addresses this request.

National Institute of Food and Agriculture

For FY2015, the House-reported bill would provide $1.274 billion for NIFA, $3 million less than the FY2014 appropriation. This reduction is effectively about $9 million because of the addition of rental expenses. The Senate bill would provide about $19 million more than the House bill, which represents a small increase over FY2014, even after the addition of rental expenses. Within the NIFA total:

- **Research and Education Activities** would receive $775 million in the House bill and $788 million in the Senate bill.

  - USDA's flagship competitive grants program—the Agriculture and Food Research Initiative (AFRI), with about one-fourth of NIFA's total budget—receives a $9 million increase to $325 million in both the House and Senate bills. This concurs with the Administration's request.

  - The Administration had requested $75 million for "Innovation Institutes," that would focus on emerging agricultural research challenges. Startup funding of $25 million per year for each of three institutes, for five years, would leverage public-private partnerships. Proposed research areas were pollinator health, bio-manufacturing and bioproducts development, and anti-microbial resistance. Neither bill would fund the institute model, although the research topics are addressed in other program funding.

- **Extension Activities** would receive $467 million in the House bill and $473 million in the Senate bill. Both amounts are within 1% of the FY2014 amount.

- **Integrated Activities**—which had declined by about two-thirds from FY2010 through FY2013 (from $60 million to $20 million) but was raised to $35 million in FY2014—would be reduced again in FY2015. The House and Senate bills are similar in proposing about $32 million to Integrated Activities for FY2015, more than the Administration's request but about 9% less than the FY2014 amount.

As part of the Administration's proposal for a government-wide reorganization of STEM programs,[31] NIFA would defund its Higher Education Challenge Grants, Graduate and Postgraduate Fellowship Grants, the Higher Education Multicultural Scholars Program, Women and Minorities in STEM Program, Agriculture in the Classroom, and Secondary and Postsecondary Challenge Grants. With the exception of the Agriculture in the Classroom program that the House bill would defund, neither the House nor Senate bill follows the Administration's proposed reorganization (both bills continue to fund these programs).

Finally, in addition to the base request for NIFA, the Administration proposed an additional $80 million through the OGS Initiative. Most of this extra amount would provide increased support for additional AFRI competitive research grants ($60 million). The rest would establish a new competitive research grant program to complement formula-funded NIFA grants. Neither the House nor Senate bill addresses this request.

National Agricultural Statistics Service

For FY2015, the House-reported bill would provide $169 million for NASS, an increase of $8.2 million over FY2014, all of which is needed to cover the $9.2 million additional cost of rental payments. The Senate-reported bill would provide $178 million, nearly $9 million more than the House proposal and at the level of the Administration's request.

Economic Research Service

For FY2015, the House-reported bill would provide $86 million, an increase of nearly $8 million over FY2014 and equal to the additional cost of rental payments. The Senate-reported bill would provide slightly less than the House bill, making the FY2014 amount effectively equal, or slightly less than, the FY2014 amount after adjusting for the addition of rental payments.

Marketing and Regulatory Programs

Three agencies carry out USDA's marketing and regulatory programs mission area: the Animal and Plant Health Inspection Service (APHIS), the Agricultural Marketing Service (AMS), and the Grain Inspection, Packers, and Stockyards Administration (GIPSA).

---

[31] CRS Report IN10011, *The Administration's Proposed STEM Education Reorganization: Where Are We Now?*

Animal and Plant Health Inspection Service[32]

The Animal and Plant Health Inspection Service (APHIS) is responsible for protecting U.S. agriculture from domestic and foreign pests and diseases, responding to domestic animal and plant health problems, and facilitating agricultural trade through science-based standards. APHIS has key responsibilities for dealing with prominent concerns such as avian influenza (AI), bovine spongiform encephalopathy (BSE or "mad cow disease"), bovine tuberculosis, a growing number of invasive plant pests—such as the Emerald Ash Borer, the Asian Long-horned Beetle, and the Glassy-winged Sharpshooter—and a national animal identification (ID) program for animal disease tracking and control. APHIS also is charged with administering the Animal Welfare Act (AWA), which seeks to protect pets and other animals used for research and entertainment.

The House bill would provide $867.5 million and the Senate bill would provide $872.4 million for APHIS salaries and expenses, which is about $35 million more than the Administration's request of $834.3 million. Both bills would provide an additional $3.2 million for buildings and facilities, and would authorize APHIS to collect fees to cover the total costs of providing technical assistance, goods, or services in certain cases.

The House and Senate FY2015 recommendations compare to the FY2014 appropriation of $821.7 million for salaries and expenses and $3.2 million for buildings and facilities. In part, higher FY2015 amounts compared to FY2014 are largely attributable to rental payments of $42.6 million to the General Services Administration (GSA) and Department of Homeland Security (DHS) that previously were funded through the Agriculture Buildings and Facilities and Rental Payments Account.

Both bills also specify in report language amounts at the program level.[33] Within APHIS, the following appropriations are provided across each of the proposed budget categories and are roughly comparable: plant health (House bill, $302.9 million; Senate bill, $303.2 million); animal health ($292.0 million; $289.4 million); wildlife services (both bills provide $109.0 million); regulatory services ($35.6 million; $34.4 million); safe trade and international technical assistance ($34.4 million; $36.2 million); animal welfare ($28.9 million; $28.7 million); emergency preparedness ($17.5 million; $17.4 million); and agency management (both bills provide $52.0 million, which includes payments to GSA and DHA mentioned previously).

As in previous years, both the House and Senate bills highlight that appropriators expect USDA to continue to use the authority provided in the appropriation and in statute to transfer funds from other appropriations or funds available to USDA for activities related to the arrest and eradication of animal and plant pests and diseases.[34] The Office of Management and Budget (OMB) and congressional appropriators have sparred for years over whether APHIS should—as appropriators have preferred—reach as needed into USDA's Commodity Credit Corporation (CCC) account for mandatory funds to deal with emerging plant pests and other plant and animal health problems on

---

[32] This section was written by Renée Johnson (7-9588; rjohnson@crs.loc.gov).

[33] Sub-account levels are according to APHIS's new budget structure proposed and implemented as part of the FY2012 appropriations process that reorganized and consolidated APHIS programs across 29 budgetary line items. For more information, see CRS Report R41964, *Agriculture and Related Agencies: FY2012 Appropriations.* See also USDA, "2012 Budget and Explanatory Notes, APHIS," pp. 18-47 through 18-50, http://www.obpa.usda.gov/18aphis2012notes.pdf.

[34] This provision is in accordance with the Animal Health Protection Act (7 U.S.C. §§ 8310 and 8316, §§10411 and 10417) and the Plant Protection Act (7 U.S.C. §§ 7751 and 7772, §§431 and 442).

an emergency basis, or be provided the funds primarily through the annual USDA appropriation, as OMB has argued. In particular, both committees highlight the need for USDA to use its authority to transfer CCC funds to address emerging plant pests. Both bills recommend that funds be made available until expended for a "contingency fund" to control outbreaks of insects, plant diseases, animal diseases and for control of pest animals and birds to the extent necessary to meet emergency conditions. The House bill recommends $0.470 million and the Senate bill recommends $0.485 million be available for this contingency fund.

The Committees on Appropriations in both the House and Senate have expressed a number of shared priorities. Both the House and Senate bills express concern about the emergence of Porcine Epidemic Diarrhea virus (PEDv) that has had a devastating impact on the U.S. hog sector over the past year. The House bill provides $3.5 million to address PEDv, consisting of $2.5 million for the swine health program and $1.0 million for the National Animal Health Laboratory Network (NAHLN) to support veterinary diagnostics. The Senate bill provides additional, but unspecified, funding for PEDv and for NAHLN. In addition, both the House and Senate appropriations committees provide increased support for the National Veterinary Stockpile as well as activities under the authority of the Horse Protection Act, and also address issues pertaining to Agricultural Quarantine and Inspection (AQI) user fees.

Both the House and Senate bills and committee reports contain provisions and language intended to address a range of animal wildlife services, damage management, and methods development, including aquaculture animal health, although in some cases differ in approach. Both express concerns about cotton pests, screw worm, Sudden Oak Death and other tree and wood pests, among other specialty crop and invasive pests, as well as issues pertaining to the brucellosis eradication program. The bills, however, differ in terms of some specific pests and diseases of concern. For example, the House bill and committee report expresses concerns about the Brown Marmorated Stink Bug, the Conehead Termite, and the Potato Cyst Nematode, and also feral swine management and cervid[35] health, among other types of emerging pests and diseases. The House bill also provides for continued support for citrus greening disease (also known as Huanglongbing) through increased funding of $5 million for the Citrus Health Response Program (CHRP). The Senate bill and committee report provides specific mention of the Asian Long-Horned Beetle, honey bee pests, chronic wasting disease, and invasive annual grasses.

Agricultural Marketing Service and "Section 32"[36]

The Agricultural Marketing Service (AMS) administers numerous programs that facilitate the marketing of U.S. agricultural products in domestic and international markets. AMS each year receives appropriations in two different ways. A discretionary appropriation of about $80 million funds a variety of marketing activities. A larger mandatory amount of about $1.1 billion ("Section 32," a.k.a. Funds for strengthening markets, income and supply) finances various types of ad-hoc decisions that support agricultural commodities (such as livestock, fruits, and vegetables) that are not supported through the direct subsidy programs for the primary field crops (corn, soybeans, wheat, cotton, rice, peanuts) and dairy.[37]

---

[35] Refers to any ruminant mammal of the family Cervidae, including deer, moose, and elk.

[36] The AMS marketing services section was written by Remy Jurenas (7-7281, rjurenas@crs.loc.gov) and the Section 32 portion by Dennis A. Shields (7-9051, dshields@crs.loc.gov).

[37] In addition, user fees and reimbursements finance other AMS-administered activities, such as product quality and (continued...)

Marketing Activities

The discretionary appropriation (8% of AMS' total FY2014 appropriated resources) funds several programs—dissemination of marketing news, collection of data on pesticide residues and sampling foods consumed by infants and children, development and revision of quality grade standards for traded commodities, analysis of issues dealing with transporting agricultural commodities, analysis and support of local food marketing efforts, implementation of the national organic program, surveillance to ensure that only eggs fit for human consumption are sold, implementation of country of origin labeling requirements for covered commodities, administration of federal regulations on the interstate shipment of agricultural and vegetable seeds, and administering matching grants to states for resolving issues.[38]

The House-reported bill (H.R. 4800) provides $82.4 million for marketing services plus payments to states and possessions, $1.1 million more (+1.4%) than made available in FY2014, but $1.8 million less (-2.1%) than requested by the Administration. House report language recommends FY2015 funding for National Organic and Pesticide Data programs be equivalent to their FY2014 levels. The Senate-reported bill (S. 2389) appropriates slightly more than does the House measure ($83.0 million).

In its report (H.Rept. 113-468), the House Appropriations Committee "directs USDA not to implement or enforce the [Country of Origin Labeling (COOL)] final rule [issued in May 2013] should the WTO [World Trade Organization] issue a final ruling against the United States." The Committee further directs the Secretary of Agriculture to "promptly issue a notice in the *Federal Register* announcing that the COOL rule is suspended until further notice if the final ruling is against the United States." As background, Canada and Mexico challenged the May 2013 rule, claiming it does not comply with earlier WTO dispute settlement findings. To pursue their case, both countries in September 2013 sought a ruling, expected to be released this fall, on this matter from a WTO compliance panel. Report language notes that U.S. exports to both countries "will suffer an economic impact" of about $2 billion "in retaliatory actions" if the WTO determines that the COOL final rule is inconsistent with U.S. obligations under various WTO trade obligations.[39]

During floor action, the House adopted H.Amdt. 856 (by a vote of 223 to 198) by Representative Royce that reduces funding for AMS by $15.5 million and shifts $10 million to the Foreign Agricultural Service (see "Local and Regional Procurement (LRP) Projects"). Final action on the amended bill has yet to take place.

(...continued)

process verification programs, commodity grading, and Perishable Agricultural Commodities Act licensing.

[38] Separate from the appropriations process, the 2014 farm bill (P.L. 113-79) authorizes mandatory funding for four AMS-administered programs as follows: $72.5 million (annually, FY2014-2017) and $85 million (annually, FY2018 and thereafter) for specialty crop block grants, $15 million (annually, FY2014-2018) for farmers' market promotion, $15 million (annually, FY2014-2018) for local food promotion, and a set-aside (estimated at $12.5 million in FY2015) for AMS share of costs to support organic certification. For FY2015, AMS expects to administer an estimated $115 million of these mandatory farm bill initiatives.

[39] For information on COOL and background on the dispute brought by Canada and Mexico challenging the implementation of this law, see CRS Report RS22955, *Country-of-Origin Labeling for Foods and the WTO Trade Dispute on Meat Labeling*.

Section 32 (Funds for strengthening markets, income and supply)

AMS's mandatory appropriation (which accounted for 92% of total agency funding in FY2014) reflects a transfer from the so-called Section 32, an appropriation created in 1935 to assist agricultural producers of non-price-supported commodities. The Section 32 account is funded by a permanent appropriation of 30% of the previous calendar year's customs receipts ($9.2 billion in FY2014), less certain mandatory transfers to child nutrition and other programs ($8.1 billion in FY2014).[40]

Section 32 monies available for obligation by AMS have been used at the Secretary's discretion to purchase agricultural commodities like meats, poultry, fruits, vegetables, and fish, which are not typically covered by mandatory farm programs. These commodities are diverted to school lunch and other domestic food and nutrition programs. Section 32 has also been used to fund surplus removal and farm economic and disaster relief activities.

The 2008 farm bill (§14222) capped the annual amount of Section 32 funds available for obligation by AMS in FY2015 at $1.284 billion. Also, to increase the amount of fruits and vegetables purchased under Section 32, Congress limited USDA's discretion in two ways: (1) §4304 of the 2008 farm bill established a fresh fruit and vegetable school snack program funded by carving out Section 32 funds (set at $40 million in 2008, rising to $150 million in 2011, and adjusted for inflation for each year thereafter), and (2) §4404 of the 2008 farm bill required additional purchases of fruits, vegetables, and nuts (set at $190 million in FY2008, rising to $206 million in FY2012, and remaining at that level each year thereafter). Section 4214 of the 2014 farm bill expanded the school snack program to include frozen, canned, and dried fruits and vegetables on a pilot basis for the 2014-15 school year.

Both the House-reported and Senate-reported FY2015 Agriculture appropriations bills provide $1.122 billion of Section 32 funds for AMS, which is the same as the Administration's request, and compares with $1.107 billion enacted in FY2014. This amount represents the actual level of funding available for obligations by AMS, after rescissions and mandatory transfers have been made, and is considered mandatory spending.

Both bills also include a provision (§718 in the House-reported bill and §719 in the Senate-reported bill) that has appeared since FY2012 that effectively prohibits the use of Section 32 for emergency disaster payments to farmers:

> [N]one of the funds appropriated or otherwise made available by this or any other Act shall be used to pay the salaries or expenses of any employee of the Department of Agriculture or officer of the Commodity Credit Corporation to carry out clause 3 of Section 32 of the Agricultural Adjustment Act of 1935 (P.L. 74-320, 7 U.S.C. 612c, as amended), or for any surplus removal activities or price support activities under section 5 of the Commodity Credit Corporation Charter Act.[41]

---

[40] For more details about Section 32 and the farm bill changes, see CRS Report RL34081, *Farm and Food Support Under USDA's Section 32 Program.*

[41] Clause 3 of Section 32 provides that funds shall be used to re-establish farmers' purchasing power by making payments in connections with the normal production of any agricultural commodity for domestic consumption (7.U.S.C 612c). Section 5 of the Commodity Credit Corporation Charter Act authorizes the CCC to support the prices of agricultural commodities through loans, purchases, payments, and other operations (15 U.S.C. 714c).

Despite this restriction, the Senate committee report language notes the importance of the ability of the Secretary to provide direct assistance, and directs the Secretary to provide notification to the Appropriations Committee in advance of any public announcement or release of Section 32 funds (§719 nonetheless restricts the Secretary's authority to use these funds for such purposes).

Grain Inspection, Packers and Stockyards Administration[42]

USDA's Grain Inspection, Packers and Stockyards Administration (GIPSA) oversees the marketing of U.S. grain, oilseeds, livestock, poultry, meat, and other commodities. GIPSA's Federal Grain Inspection Service establishes standards for the inspection, weighing, and grading of grain, rice, and other commodities. The Packers and Stockyards Program monitors livestock and poultry markets to ensure fair competition and guard against deceptive and fraudulent trade practices.

The House-reported FY2015 Agriculture appropriations bill (H.R. 4800) provides $43.7 million for GIPSA salaries and expenses, which is $3.5 million (+8.6%) more than the amount enacted for FY2014. The Senate-reported FY2015 Agriculture appropriations bill (S. 2389) provides $44.0 million, $3.8 million (+9.3%) more than for FY2014. The House bill provides $0.3 million less than (-0.7%) the Administration's budget request, but the Senate bill matches the request. Both the House and Senate appropriations bills authorize GIPSA to collect up to $50 million in user fees for inspection and weighing services. GIPSA may exceed the user fee limit by 10% to cover unexpected inspection and weighing costs if the Committees on Appropriations are notified.

Section 730 of the House-reported bill restricts USDA from finalizing or implementing parts of the GIPSA proposed rule on livestock and poultry marketing practices (75 Federal Register 35338, June 22, 2010; amends 9 C.F.R. Part 201) that were required in the 2008 farm bill (P.L. 110-246).[43] The proposed rule addresses how competitive injury is treated under the Packers and Stockyard Act (P&S Act; 7 U.S.C. §181 et seq.), sets criteria for determining unfair, unjustly discriminatory and deceptive practices, and undue or unreasonable preference or advantages; and includes arbitration provisions that give contract growers opportunities to participate in meaningful arbitration. The proposed rule was contentious, with proponents arguing that it would bring fairness to marketing transactions, while opponents argued it would disrupt markets and lead to increased litigation. USDA finalized parts of the proposed rule in December 2011, but much of the rule was not finalized because prohibitions have been enforced in appropriations acts since FY2012.

Section 730 allows USDA to publish a final or interim final GIPSA rule only if the annual cost to the economy is less than $100 million. Also, it prohibits USDA from using any funds to implement specific provisions that were in the proposed rule. They are the definitions of the tournament system §201.2(l); competitive injury §201.2(t); and the likelihood of injury §201.2(u). Other prohibited parts include the applicability of the regulations on conduct that is a violation of the P&S Act §201.3(c); unfair, unjust discriminatory and deceptive practices §201.210; undue or unreasonable preferences §201.211; livestock and poultry contracts §201.213; and the tournament system §201.214. In addition, the section rescinds funding for the enforcement of three provisions

---

[42] This section was written by Joel L. Greene (7-9877, jgreene@crs.loc.gov).

[43] For more, see CRS Report R41673, *USDA's "GIPSA Rule" on Livestock and Poultry Marketing Practices*.

that USDA finalized in 2011. They are the definition of suspension of delivery of birds §201.2(o), the applicability to live poultry §201.3(a), and the 90-day notification for suspension of delivery of birds §210.215(a).

The Senate appropriations bill does not include a provision on the GIPSA proposed rule.

Food Safety[44]

Numerous federal, state, and local agencies share responsibilities for regulating the safety of the U.S. food supply.[45] Federal responsibility for food safety rests primarily with the Food and Drug Administration (FDA) and the USDA. FDA, an agency of the Department of Health and Human Services, is responsible for ensuring the safety of the majority of all domestic and imported food products (except for meat and poultry products).[46] USDA's Food Safety and Inspection Service (FSIS) regulates most meat, poultry, and processed egg products.[47] The agriculture appropriations subcommittees oversee both the FDA and FSIS budgets.

Historically, federal funding and staffing levels between FDA and FSIS have been disproportionate to their respective responsibilities for addressing food safety activities. Although FSIS is responsible for roughly 10%-20% of the U.S. food supply, it has received about 60% of the two agencies' combined food safety budget. Although FDA has been responsible for 80%-90% of the U.S. food supply, a few years ago it received about 40% of the combined budget for federal food safety activities (**Table 5**). Staffing levels also have varied considerably among the two agencies: FSIS staff numbered around 9,400 FTEs in FY2010, while FDA staff working on food-related activities numbers about 3,400 FTEs.

In recent years, however, the balance of overall funding for food safety between FDA and USDA has started to shift. Congressional appropriators have increased funding for FDA food activities, which more than doubled from $435.5 million in FY2005 to $882.8 million in FY2014 (**Table 5**). Funding for FSIS remained mostly unchanged to slightly lower overall. The Food Safety Modernization Act (FSMA) also provided for additional limited funding through certain types of industry-paid user fees.

FSMA—comprehensive food safety legislation enacted in the 111th Congress—authorized additional appropriations and staff for FDA's future food safety activities.[48] FSMA was the largest expansion of FDA's food safety authorities since the 1930s. Among its many provisions, FSMA authorized increasing frequency of inspections at food facilities, tightening record-keeping requirements, extending oversight to certain farms, and also mandated product recalls. It requires food processing, manufacturing, shipping, and other facilities to conduct a food safety plan of the most likely safety hazards, and design and implement risk-based controls. It also mandates

---

[44] This section was written by Renée Johnson (7-9588; rjohnson@crs.loc.gov), with contributions from Joel Greene (FSIS) and Susan Thaul (FDA Foods Program).

[45] For more information, see CRS Report RS22600, *The Federal Food Safety System: A Primer*.

[46] FDA's food safety authorities rest primarily with the Federal Food, Drug, and Cosmetic Act (FFDCA, 21 U.S.C. §§301 *et seq.*).

[47] Laws governing FSIS include the Federal Meat Inspection Act (FMIA, 21 U.S.C. §§601, *et seq.*), the Poultry Products Inspection Act (PPIA, 21 U.S.C. §§451, *et seq.*), and the Egg Products Inspection Act (EPIA, 21 U.S.C. §§1031, *et seq.*).

[48] P.L. 111-353 amended the Federal Food, Drug, and Cosmetic Act (FFDCA).

improvements to the nation's foodborne illness surveillance systems and increased scrutiny of food imports, among other provisions. FSMA did not directly address meat and poultry products under USDA's jurisdiction.

Although Congress authorized appropriations when it enacted FSMA, it did not provide the funding needed for FDA to perform these activities. After FSMA was signed into law in January 2011, concerns were voiced about whether there would be enough money to overhaul the U.S. food safety system and also whether expanded investment in this area was appropriate in the current budgetary climate.[49] Prior to enactment, the Congressional Budget Office (CBO) estimated that implementing FSMA could increase net federal spending subject to appropriation by about $1.4 billion over a five-year period (FY2011-FY2015).[50] This cost estimate covers activities at FDA and other federal agencies, and does not include offsetting revenue from the collection of new user fees authorized under FSMA.[51] FSMA did not impose any new facility registration fees. Prior to enactment, CBO estimated that about $240 million in new fees would be collected over the five-year period (FY2011-FY2015).[52] Taking into account these new fees, CBO estimated that covering the five-year cost of new requirements within FDA, including more frequent inspections, would require additional outlays of $1.1 billion. FSMA also authorized an increase in FDA staff, which was expected to reach 5,000 by FY2014.[53] Instead, FDA reports actual staffing levels at 3,800 FTEs in FY2014 (**Table 5**).

FDA continues to implement regulations under FSMA. Although Congress has added to FDA's budget for its Foods Program in the past few years, agency officials claim it will need an additional $400 million to $450 million more per year above its FY2012 base to fully implement FSMA.[54]

---

[49] See "Food Safety Bill Advocates Expect Funding Fight," *Food Safety News*, January 4, 2011.

[50] CBO, Cost Estimate, "S. 510, Food Safety Modernization Act, as reported by the Senate Committee on Health, Education, Labor, and Pensions on December 18, 2009, incorporating a manager's amendment released on August 12, 2010," August 12, 2010, http://www.cbo.gov/ftpdocs/117xx/doc11794/s510.pdf; reflects the Senate amendment to S. 510. Estimated total costs would be covered by a combination of user fees and direct appropriations (budget authority).

[51] FSMA authorized additional appropriations and staff for FDA's future food safety activities and authorized new user fees. New fees authorized under FSMA include an annual fee for participants in the voluntary qualified importer program (VQIP) and three fees for certain periodic activities involving reinspection, recall, and export certification. FSMA, P.L. 111-353, §§107 and 401. Details of these annual and periodic fees are presented in CRS Report R40443, *The FDA Food Safety Modernization Act (P.L. 111-353)*.

[52] As estimated by CBO, these fees would be phased in as follows: $15 million (FY2011), $27 million (FY2012); $47 million (FY2013); $63 million (FY2014); and $89 million (FY2015).

[53] FSMA, P.L. 111-353, §401. By fiscal year, staff level increases were authorized to a total of not fewer than: 4,000 staff members (FY2011); 4,200 staff (FY2012); 4,600 staff (FY2013); and 5,000 staff (FY2014).

[54] FDA, *Building Domestic Capacity to Implement the FDA Food Safety Modernization Act (FSMA)*, May 2013.

Table 5. Food Safety Appropriations

(FTEs as indicated, and budget and appropriation figures in millions of dollars)

Agency/Year	FTEs[a]	Appropriation[b]	Program Level, Including Fees[c]
HHS Food and Drug Administration (FDA), "Foods" Subtotal			
FY2009 Actual	2,995	712.8	712.8
FY2010 Actual	3,387	783.2	783.2
FY2011 Actual	3,605	836.2	836.2
FY2012 Actual	3,546	866.1	882.7
FY2013 Operating Plan (post-sequestration)	3,626	796.6[d]	813.2
FY2014, Appropriation (P.L. 113-76)	3,805	882.8	900.3
FY2015: Administration Request	4,236	903.4	1,124.3[e]
H.R. 4800, as reported	NA	903.4	913.8
FY2015, S. 2389, as reported	NA	903.4	913.8
USDA Food Safety and Inspection Service (FSIS)			
FY2009 Actual	9,343	971.6	1,105.7
FY2010 Actual	9,401	1,018.5	1,172.4
FY2011 Actual	9,465	1,008.5	1,187.2
FY2012 Actual	9,351	1,004.4	1,169.1
FY2013 Operating Plan (post-sequestration)	9,158	977.3[f]	1,163.7
FY2014, Appropriation (P.L. 113-76)	9,360	1,010.7	1,183.2
FY2015: Administration Request	9,098	1,001.4	1,174.9
FY2015, H.R. 4800, as reported	NA	1,005.2	NA
FY2015, S. 2389, as reported	NA	1,022.8	NA

Sources: CRS, from H.R. 4800, S. 2389, FDA FY2013 Sequestration Operating Plan, FDA FY2014 Operating Plan, and annual agency budget justifications for FDA (http://www.fda.gov/AboutFDA/ReportsManualsForms/Reports/BudgetReports/default.htm) and FSIS (http://www.obpa.usda.gov/explan_notes.html). NA=not available.

Notes:

a. Staffing in full time equivalents (FTEs).

b. Does not include existing or proposed user fees or other 'non-federal' payments.

c. Includes user fees. For FDA, reflects actual or planned fees through FY2014, and for FY2015. enacted, CR, and requested fee amounts. For FSIS, includes existing fees and trust fund for overtime, holiday, and voluntary inspection.

d. FDA's "FY2013 Sequestration Operating Plan." and "FY2014 Operating Plan."

e. The Administration's requested Foods program level total includes $10.4 million in authorized fees relating to food reinspection, food and feed recall, and the voluntary qualified importer program; and other proposed fees covering food facility registration and inspection, food import, international courier, and food contact notification fees. The "Appropriation" amount excludes fees (both authorized and proposed) from the requested "Program Level" amount.

f. Reported by USDA for FSIS in its "Fiscal Year 2013 Operating Plan" and reflects "2013 Enacted w/ Sequester and Rescissions."

Food and Drug Administration (FDA)

FDA's foods program accounts for about one-third of the agency's total budget authority.[55] For FDA's foods program, both the House- and Senate-reported bills would provide $903.4 million in federal appropriations for FY2015 (**Table 5**). These congressional appropriations are expected to be augmented by existing (currently authorized) user fees. A total program level, including appropriations and fees, would be $913.8 million. These fees, as authorized under FSMA, include food and feed recall fees, food reinspection fees, and voluntary qualified importer program fees.

The House and Senate recommended total program level funding (appropriations plus user fees) is $210.5 million below the Administration's request, which proposed several new user fees not authorized by Congressional appropriators (**Table 5**). In addition to FSMA-authorized use fees, the Administration's budget also requests approval of other new user fees. These proposed fees included a food facility registration and inspection, food import, international courier, and food contact notification fees. Neither the House nor the Senate appropriations bills include the Administration's proposed fees. The House committee report broadly addresses FDA user fees, requesting a report on user fees collected for each user fee program.

Both the House and Senate appropriators make a number of recommendations regarding FSMA and FDA's ongoing efforts to develop regulations and guidance pertaining to the various provisions of the law. Both address FSMA's re-proposal of certain key regulations regarding food safety preventive controls for both human and animal food, and also produce standards.[56] The House committee report expresses concern that FDA is taking an "overly prescriptive regulatory approach" with many of the regulations including the monitoring of preventive controls and verification testing activities, and urges FDA to "ensure all FSMA regulations are risk-based, flexible, and science-based, and embrace the well-established and recognized standards for food safety already employed through much of the industry." The Senate committee report further expresses concern that FDA "only intends to address discrete portions of these proposed rules" and reminds the agency that the activities covered by FSMA's rules are "complex and interrelated" and any regulations need to be "science-based, risk-based, and flexible, taking into account the different risks posed by different commodities." The example provided includes the need to consider the "secondary market for spent grains and byproduct from human food manufacturing and agricultural practices" that is often used for animal feed. The House committee report also directs FDA to ensure that all FDA centers (including the Foods Program) maintain a "firm commitment to science-based, data-driven decision making, facilitating the free flow of scientific and technical information, and requiring a fair and transparent approach to resolving scientific disputes."

House appropriators furthermore maintain FY2014 funding levels of $25 million for food safety activities such as the "development of guidance, providing technical assistance to industry and technical support to FDA inspectors, as well as training for FDA and state inspectors." The House committee encourages FDA to consider "funding research that would provide portable and technologically advanced testing platforms needed to effectively monitor and protect against intentional adulteration of the food supply," as part of the National Agriculture and Food Defense Strategy Plan, as required by FSMA. The House also urges FDA to consider exempting tree nut producers from the produce standards rule, if the tree nuts meet the criteria for "rarely consumed

---

[55] The entirety of FDA appropriations is discussed later in "Food and Drug Administration (FDA)" and **Table 11**.

[56] For more information, see CRS Report R42885, *Food Safety Issues for the 113th Congress.*

raw" and the buyer of the tree nuts takes the necessary steps to reduce pathogens as described in the proposed FSMA rule.

Both the House and Senate committees encourage FDA to form partnerships under FSMA. House appropriators encourage FDA to "work in partnership with existing government food safety programs through Memorandum of Understandings to verify compliance with FSMA" and to "eliminate duplication of activities under the law." Senate appropriators emphasize the need for FDA to work with USDA to "perform outreach and technical assistance to farmers and small businesses" and recommend $2.5 million in funding for USDA's National Institute of Food and Agriculture (NIFA) to conduct extension activities related to FSMA. Appropriators also emphasize the importance of ensuring adequate public review and comment on all proposed requirements and supporting analyses. The House report expresses concern that FDA is not providing stakeholders with "adequate input or economic consideration on an expanding list of highly technical regulatory proposals" and wants the agency to better manage its priorities, given certain gaps in the regulatory process involving some FSMA rules.

Both the House and Senate committee reports contain provisions related to seafood safety, and direct FDA to publish updated advice to pregnant women on seafood consumption.[57] The Senate report further encourages FDA to "work with States and the Department of Commerce to more aggressively combat fraud in parts of the seafood industry."[58] FDA is also encouraged to work with the U.S. Trade Representative (USTR) to resolve a dispute between the U.S. and the European Union over sanitation protocols on U.S. shellfish, and to report to Congress on this issue. The Senate also directs FDA to spend "not less than $150,000" to "implement a labeling requirement that genetically engineered salmon offered for sale to consumers" be labeled as such.

Both House and Senate appropriators broadly encourage FDA to expedite the import clearance process, and report statistics to Congress that measure the effectiveness of targeting resources and to clear trusted/compliant shipments. The House committee also requires FDA to report to Congress on its investigation involving imported pet food, including providing a summary of recent activities, as well as an annual report on the status of the investigation.

Finally, both House and Senate appropriators urge FDA to devise strategies to address the use of medically important antibiotics in food animals. The House report further encourages FDA to maintain appropriate funding levels for both FSMA-related activities and the base work performed by its food and veterinary medicine programs and through research with their Centers of Excellence.

Food Safety and Inspection Service (FSIS)

For USDA's FSIS, the House-reported bill (H.R. 4800) provides $1.005 billion in federal appropriations for FY2015, while the Senate-reported appropriations bill (S. 2389) provides $1.023 billion (**Table 5**). These congressional appropriations are expected to be augmented by existing (currently authorized) user fees, which FSIS had earlier estimated would total approximately $150 million.[59] Both bills allocate FSIS appropriations between various sub-

---

[57] FDA recently published draft updated advice on fish consumption. See FDA, "FDA and EPA issue draft updated advice for fish consumption," FDA News Release, June 10, 2014.

[58] CRS Report R43358, *Food Fraud and "Economically Motivated Adulteration" of Food and Food Ingredients.*

[59] FSIS congressional budget justification (http://www.obpa.usda.gov/explan_notes html).

accounts for federal, state, and international inspection; Codex Alimentarius; and the Public Health Data Communications Infrastructure System. Differences between the House and Senate bills are attributable to higher recommended appropriations for both federal and state inspections in the Senate bill.

The Administration requested $1.001 billion for FSIS for FY2015. The Administration also proposed a user fee of $4 million to cover additional inspection costs associated with performance issues at inspected establishments. Neither appropriations bill included the user fee proposal.

Both the House and Senate bills provide that $1 million may be credited from fees collected for the cost of the national laboratory accreditation programs,[60] and require that no fewer than 148 FTEs be dedicated to the inspection and enforcement of the Humane Methods of Slaughter Act (HMSA) during FY2015. The Senate-reported bill requires that FSIS continue to implement catfish inspection as required under the 2008 and 2014 farm bills.[61] The House bill does not contain similar language.

Both committee reports further address additional issues regarding animal welfare. The House report requires that inspectors hired with funding previously specified for HMSA enforcement oversee compliance with humane handling rules for live animals. The Senate report directs FSIS to continue to provide annual reports to the appropriations committee on the implementation of objective scoring methods for enforcing the HMSA.

Both committee reports also prohibit FSIS from paying the salaries and expenses to inspect horses for slaughter or to provide voluntary, fee-for-service inspection of horses.[62] During FY2006 and FY2007 appropriations acts prohibited FSIS from paying salaries and expenses for horse slaughter inspections. From FY2008 to FY2011, the appropriations acts also banned voluntary, fee-based horse slaughter inspections. The appropriations ban on horse inspections was not in appropriations acts for FY2012 and FY2013, but is in force for FY2014. No horse slaughter facilities opened before the ban was reinstated in FY2014.

Both committee reports also support FSIS efforts to encourage water-saving technologies in slaughter and processing facilities. The House report urges FSIS to work with Tribes to establish a voluntary program for slaughtering buffalo and bison. The Senate report expresses disappointment that FSIS has not finalized a catfish inspection rule and directs FSIS to implement all domestic and import inspections no later than one year after the enactment of the Agricultural Act of 2014, which would be Feb. 7, 2015.

---

[60] Authorized by §1327 of the Food, Agriculture, Conservation and Trade Act of 1990 (7 U.S.C. 138f).

[61] P.L. 110-246, §11016, clarified in P.L. 113-79, §12106.

[62] H.R. 4800, § 741; S. 2389, § 746.

Farm Service Agency[63]

USDA's Farm Service Agency (FSA) is probably best known for administering the farm commodity subsidy programs and the disaster assistance programs. It makes these payments to farmers through a network of county offices. In addition, FSA also administers USDA's direct and guaranteed farm loan programs, certain mandatory conservation programs (in cooperation with the Natural Resources Conservation Service), and supports certain international food assistance and export credit programs administered by the Foreign Agricultural Service and the U.S. Agency for International Development.

FSA Salaries and Expenses

For FY2015, the House-reported bill would provide $1.512 billion to FSA for salaries and expenses (**Table 6**, including amounts for regular FSA salaries and expenses, plus the transfer within FSA for the salaries and expenses of the farm loan program).[64] This is $27.1 million more than the amount for FY2014, and the increase equals the amount for building rental payments that the agency is becoming responsible for in FY2015 (see "Departmental Administration"). Thus, after adjusting for the new rental expenses, the House bill would be level with FY2014.

The Senate bill for FY2015 would provide $1.490 billion to FSA for salaries and expenses. This is $22.5 million less than the House bill and about $5 million more than FY2014. After the addition of rental expenses in FY2015, the Senate bill is a slight reduction compared to FY2014.

Both the House and Senate reports criticize FSA for delays and costs in implementing the MIDAS (Modernize and Innovate the Delivery of Agricultural Systems) computer upgrade process. MIDAS was flagged for concern by the IT Dashboard in December 2012. It has struggled with the scope and schedule of work, and has yet to achieve the expected results.[65] The Government Accountability Office also observed management and schedule problems in 2011.[66]

Both of the FY2015 appropriations bills—in the Senate bill text[67] and in both bills' committee reports[68]—reject USDA's proposal to close 250 FSA county offices and reduce staffing. They cite insufficient information, justification, and/or poor timing regarding implementing the 2014 farm bill. This is the first time that FSA office closure has been mentioned in appropriations since FY2006-FY2008, which limited FSA's ability to close offices. The 2008 farm bill enacted a permanent provision (7 USC 6932a; P.L. 110-246, sec. 14212) that accomplished the same thing—setting conditions and requiring congressional notification and local hearings before FSA can close or consolidate a county office. The workload evaluation mentioned in the FY2015 committee reports was in the House-proposed 2014 farm bill, but was not adopted in conference.

---

[63] This section was written by Jim Monke (7-9664, jmonke@crs.loc.gov).

[64] Excludes transfers to FSA from the Foreign Agricultural Service for administrative support (about $3 million).

[65] IT Dashboard, "Farm Program Modernization (MIDAS) #097," at https://itdashboard.gov/investment?buscid=225.

[66] GAO, "USDA Systems Modernization: Management and Oversight Improvements Are Needed," GAO-11-586, July 20, 2011, at http://www.gao.gov/assets/330/321447.pdf.

[67] S. 2389 states, "That none of the funds available to the Farm Service Agency shall be used to close Farm Service Agency county offices," and that FSA cannot relocate county-based employees without congressional approval.

[68] H.Rept. 113-468 states that, "[I]n addition to the requirements mandated by the 2008 farm bill for office closures, the Department is directed to conduct, complete, and submit an evaluation of workload assessments for proposed office closures to the Committees on Appropriations ... prior to the closure of any FSA county offices."

Table 6. Farm Service Agency Appropriations
(budget authority in millions of dollars)

	FY2012 P.L. 112-55	FY2013 P.L. 113-6 post-sequ.	FY2014 P.L. 113-76	FY2015 Admin. Request	FY2015 House-reported	FY2015 Senate-reported	Change from FY2014 to House $	%	Change from House to Senate $	%
Salaries and expenses										
Farm Service Agency (S&E base)	1,199.0	1,115.3	1,177.9	1,139.3	1,205.1	1,182.5	+27.1	+2.3%	-22.5	-1.9%
FSA farm loan program S&E transfer	289.7	281.6	307.0	307.0	307.0	307.0	+0.0	+0.0%	+0.0	+0.0%
Subtotal, appropriated to FSA	**1,488.7**	**1,396.8**	**1,484.9**	**1,446.3**	**1,512.1**	**1,489.5**	**+27.1**	**+1.8%**	**-22.5**	**-1.5%**
Programs										
Farm loan program (loan subsidy)	108.2	90.5	90.0	81.2	78.7	81.2	-11.3	-12.5%	+2.5	+3.2%
Farm loan program admin. expenses	7.9	7.3	7.7	7.9	7.9	7.9	+0.2	+2.6%	+0.0	+0.0%
State mediation grants	3.8	4.1	3.8	3.4	3.4	3.4	-0.4	-10.0%	+0.0	+0.0%
Grassroots source water protection	3.8	5.2	5.5	0.0	2.5	6.5	-3.0	-54.8%	+4.0	+160.0%
Dairy indemnity program (M)	0.1	0.1	0.3	0.5	0.5	0.5	+0.3	+100.0%	+0.0	+0.0%
Total: Appropriation to FSA	**1,612.5**	**1,503.9**	**1,592.2**	**1,539.4**	**1,605.1**	**1,589.1**	**+12.9**	**+0.8%**	**-16.0**	**-1.0%**

Source: CRS, compiled from tables in the joint explanatory statements or committee reports for S. 2389, H.R. 4800, P.L. 113-76, and P.L. 112-55. Post-sequestration amounts for FY2013 are from the USDA FY2013 Operating Plan.

Notes: Does not include about $3 million of salaries and expenses that are appropriated to the Foreign Agricultural Service to administer P.L. 480 and export loans and transferred to FSA.

FSA Farm Loan Programs

The USDA Farm Service Agency makes and guarantees loans to farmers, and is a lender of last resort for family farmers unable to obtain credit from a commercial lender. USDA provides direct farm loans (loans made directly from USDA to farmers), and it also guarantees the timely repayment of principal and interest on qualified loans to farmers from commercial lenders. FSA loans are used to finance farm real estate, operating expenses, and recovery from natural disasters. Some loans are made at a low interest rate.[69]

An appropriation is made to FSA each year to cover the federal cost of making direct and guaranteed loans, referred to as a loan subsidy. Loan subsidy is directly related to any interest rate subsidy provided by the government, as well as a projection of anticipated loan losses from farmer non-repayment of the loans. The amount of loans that can be made—the loan authority— is several times larger than the subsidy level.

For FY2015, the House bill concurs with the Administration's request for the farm loan program, except that the House bill does not fund the Individual Development Account program.[70]

The House bill would provide $79 million of loan subsidy to support $6.402 billion of direct and guaranteed loans (**Table 7**). Though the loan subsidy is about 12% smaller than in FY2014, the loan authority is $875 million greater than FY2014 (+16%). Both of these changes are largely explained by the direct farm ownership program, which becomes self-supporting (through fees) and more than doubles in size. Reductions in the guaranteed operating loan program make up most of the rest of the difference.

The Senate bill would provide $81 million of loan subsidy (including the $2.5 million requested for the Individual Development Account program) to support the same $6.402 billion of direct and guaranteed loan authority as the House-reported bill and Administration request.

Following the global financial crisis that began in 2008, FSA farm loan authority generally has risen, reflecting the borrowing needs of many farmers. Broad financial system pressures dramatically increased the demand for FSA farm loans and guarantees when commercial bank lending standards became stricter and loans sometimes were less available. In FY2009 and FY2010, supplemental appropriations increased regular FSA loan authority by nearly $1 billion each year in order to meet demand, up from pre-crisis levels of about $3.5 billion in 2008 to post-supplemental levels of $6.0 billion in FY2010. From FY2011-FY2013, loan authority decreased both due to federal budget pressures and somewhat lessened demand as the financial system stabilized. Nonetheless, in some years, continued high farm loan demand for certain programs has caused the loan authority to be exhausted.[71] The FY2014 loan authority restored the total closer to the supplemental levels of FY2009 and FY2010, and the FY2015 appropriation would increase total loan authority to a new high level, particularly in the direct farm ownership loan program.

---

[69] For more background, see CRS Report RS21977, *Agricultural Credit: Institutions and Issues*.

[70] The Individual Development Account program was authorized in the 2008 farm bill, but has never been funded. It is not a loan program, but rather a savings program (7 U.S.C. 1983b). USDA grants would be matched, and farmer deposits would be augmented at a rate up to 2:1. Withdrawals could be used for various capital expenses.

[71] Updates on unused FSA loan availability are available at http://www.fsa.usda.gov/FSA/webapp?area=home& subject=fmlp&topic=fun.

Table 7. Farm Service Agency: Farm Loan Program

(budget authority and loan authority, as specified, in millions of dollars)

	FY2012	FY2013	FY2014	FY2015			Change from FY2014 to House		Change from House to Senate	
	P.L. 112-55	P.L. 113-6 post-sequ.	P.L. 113-76	Admin. Request	House-reported	Senate-reported	$	%	$	%
I. Budget Authority (loan subsidy)										
Farm ownership loans										
Direct	22.8	18.6	4.4	0.0	0.0	0.0	-4.4	-100.0%	+0.0	+0.0%
Farm operating loans										
Direct	59.1	54.0	65.5	63.1	63.1	63.1	-2.4	-3.7%	+0.0	+0.0%
Guaranteed (unsubsidized)	26.1	16.5	18.3	14.8	14.8	14.8	-3.5	-19.3%	+0.0	+0.0%
Other direct loans										
Emergency loans		1.2	1.7	0.9	0.9	0.9	-0.8	-49.6%	+0.0	+0.0%
Indian highly fractionated land loans	0.2	0.2	0.1	0.0	0.0	0.0	-0.1	-100.0%	+0.0	+0.0%
Individual Development Accounts				2.5	0.0	2.5	+0.0	+0.0%	+2.5	+0.0%
Subtotal, loan subsidy	**108.2**	**90.5**	**90.0**	**81.2**	**78.7**	**81.2**	**-11.3**	**-12.5%**	**+2.5**	**+3.2%**
FLP salaries and expenses	289.7	281.6	307.0	307.0	307.0	307.0	+0.0	+0.0%	+0.0	+0.0%
FLP administrative expenses	7.9	7.3	7.7	7.9	7.9	7.9	+0.2	+2.6%	+0.0	+0.0%
Total, FLP budget authority	**405.8**	**379.3**	**404.7**	**396.1**	**393.6**	**396.1**	**-11.1**	**-2.7%**	**+2.5**	**+0.6%**

2. Loan Authority (loan level)

| | FY2012 | FY2013 | FY2014 | FY2015 | | | Change from FY2014 to House | | Change from House to Senate | |
	P.L. 112-55	P.L. 113-6 post-sequ.	P.L. 113-76	Admin. Request	House-reported	Senate-reported	$	%	$	%
Farm ownership loans										
Direct	475.0	438.5	575.0	1,500.0	1,500.0	1,500.0	+925.0	+160.9%	+0.0	+0.0%
Guaranteed	1,500.0	1,500.0	2,000.0	2,000.0	2,000.0	2,000.0	+0.0	+0.0%	+0.0	+0.0%
Farm operating loans										
Direct	1,050.1	969.5	1,195.6	1,252.0	1,252.0	1,252.0	+56.4	+4.7%	+0.0	+0.0%
Guaranteed (unsubsidized)	1,500.0	1,384.8	1,500.0	1,393.4	1,393.4	1,393.4	-106.6	-7.1%	+0.0	+0.0%
Conservation loans										
Guaranteed	150.0	150.0	150.0	150.0	150.0	150.0	+0.0	+0.0%	+0.0	+0.0%
Other direct loans										
Emergency loans	0.0	21.6	34.7	34.7	34.7	34.7	+0.0	+0.0%	+0.0	+0.0%
Indian tribe land acquisition loans	2.0	2.0	2.0	2.0	2.0	2.0	+0.0	+0.0%	+0.0	+0.0%
Indian highly fractionated land loans	10.0	9.2	10.0	10.0	10.0	10.0	+0.0	+0.0%	+0.0	+0.0%
Boll weevil eradication loans	100.0	100.0	60.0	60.0	60.0	60.0	+0.0	+0.0%	+0.0	+0.0%
Total, loan authority	**4,787.1**	**4,575.7**	**5,527.3**	**6,402.1**	**6,402.1**	**6,402.1**	**+874.8**	**+15.8%**	**+0.0**	**+0.0%**

Source: CRS, compiled from tables in the joint explanatory statements or committee reports for S. 2389, H.R. 4800, P.L. 113-76, and P.L. 112-55. Post-sequestration amounts for FY2013 are from the USDA FY2013 Operating Plan.

Note: *Budget authority* reflects the cost of making loans, such as interest rate subsidies and default. Some programs are self-funding because of fees charged. *Loan authority* reflects the amount of loans that FSA may make or guarantee.

Commodity Credit Corporation[72]

The Commodity Credit Corporation (CCC) is the funding mechanism for most mandatory programs in the 2014 farm bill (P.L. 113-79, the Agricultural Act of 2014).[73] These include farm subsidy and disaster payments, as well as a host of other programs that receive mandatory funding such as conservation, trade, food aid, research, rural development, and bioenergy. (Programs with different mandatory funding sources than the CCC include crop insurance, SNAP, child nutrition, and Section 32.) Emergency supplemental spending also has been paid from the CCC over the years, particularly for *ad hoc* farm disaster payments, for direct market loss payments to growers of various commodities in response to low farm commodity prices, and for animal and plant disease eradication efforts. Farm Service Agency salaries and expenses (a discretionary appropriation) pays for administration of the programs.

The CCC is a wholly owned government corporation that has the legal authority to borrow up to $30 billion at any one time from the U.S. Treasury (15 U.S.C. 714 *et seq.*). These borrowed funds finance program spending, and CCC eventually must repay the funds. It may earn a small amount of money from activities such as buying and selling commodities and receiving interest payments on loans. But because the CCC never earns more than it spends, its borrowing authority must be replenished periodically through a congressional appropriation so that it does not reach its $30 billion debt limit. Congress generally provides this infusion through the annual Agriculture appropriations act. The congressional appropriation may not always restore the line of credit to the previous year's level, or may repay more than was spent. For these reasons, the appropriation to the CCC may not reflect outlays. Also, the appropriation for CCC is several billion dollars greater than the amount of farm commodity subsidies because many conservation and other mandatory programs are paid using CCC funds.[74]

To replenish CCC's borrowing authority with the Treasury, the FY2015 House-reported and Senate-reported bills concur with the Administration request for an indefinite appropriation ("such sums as necessary") for CCC. The amount is estimated in all cases to be $9.1 billion for FY2015, down 28% from FY2014. The reduction is due in part to the 2014 farm bill's elimination of "direct payments" to farmers and landowners and the delayed timing of 2014-crop farm program payments, which are scheduled to be issued in FY2016.

Mandatory outlays for the commodity programs rise and fall based on economic or weather conditions (e.g., crop prices below program trigger levels generate farm payments). Funding needs are difficult to estimate, which is a primary reason that the programs are mandatory rather than discretionary.

---

[72] This section was written by Dennis A. Shields (7-9051, dshields@crs.loc.gov).

[73] For more information on the provisions of the farm bill, see CRS Report IF00014, *The 2014 Farm Bill (Agricultural Act of 2014, P.L. 113-79) (In Focus)* and CRS Report R43076, *The 2014 Farm Bill (P.L. 113-79): Summary and Side-by-Side.*

[74] For an example of the accounting of CCC's line of credit, appropriations and expenditures, see USDA, *Commodity Estimates Book: FY2014 President's Budget*, "Output 07-CCC Financing Status," at http://www.fsa.usda.gov/Internet/FSA_File/pb14_table_07a.pdf.

Regarding authority for ad-hoc disaster assistance, both bills include a provision (§718 in the House-reported bill and §719 in the Senate-reported bill) that has appeared since FY2012 that effectively prohibits the use of CCC funds for emergency disaster payments to farmers:

> [N]one of the funds appropriated or otherwise made available by this or any other Act shall be used to pay the salaries or expenses of any employee of the Department of Agriculture or officer of the Commodity Credit Corporation to carry out clause 3 of Section 32 of the Agricultural Adjustment Act of 1935 (P.L. 74-320, 7 U.S.C. 612c, as amended), or for any surplus removal activities or price support activities under section 5 of the Commodity Credit Corporation Charter Act.[75]

Separately, only the House-reported bill would continue a provision (§725) that has been enacted since FY2011 that limits the ability of USDA to provide marketing assistance loans for mohair. Indeed, USDA has suspended the marketing loan and deficiency payment program for mohair since FY2011.[76]

Crop Insurance[77]

The federal crop insurance program is administered by USDA's Risk Management Agency (RMA). It offers basically free catastrophic insurance to producers who grow an insurable crop. Producers who opt for this coverage have the opportunity to purchase additional insurance coverage at a subsidized rate (ranging between 38% and 80%). Policies are sold and serviced through approved private insurance companies that have their program losses reinsured by USDA and are reimbursed by the government for their administrative and operating expenses.

The annual Agriculture appropriations bill traditionally makes two separate appropriations for the federal crop insurance program. First, it provides discretionary funding for the salaries and expenses of the RMA. Second, it provides "such sums as are necessary" of mandatory funding for the Federal Crop Insurance Fund, which finances all other expenses of the program, including premium subsidies, net indemnity payments, and reimbursements to the private insurance companies.

For the discretionary salaries and expenses of the RMA, the FY2015 House- and Senate-reported bills would provide approximately $77 million (same as the Administration's request), up nearly $6 million from the enacted FY2014 amount. About one-half of the increase would replace payments to the General Services Administration for rent and for payments to the Department of Homeland Security for building security activities, which was previously funded through the

---

[75] Clause 3 of Section 32 provides that funds shall be used to re-establish farmers' purchasing power by making payments in connections with the normal production of any agricultural commodity for domestic consumption (7.U.S.C 612c). Section 5 of the Commodity Credit Corporation Charter Act authorizes the CCC to support the prices of agricultural commodities through loans, purchases, payments, and other operations (15 U.S.C. 714c).

[76] USDA Farm Service Agency, Notice LP-2157, "Suspension of MAL's and LDP's for Mohair," April 15, 2011, at http://www.fsa.usda.gov/Internet/FSA_Notice/lp_2157.pdf; USDA Farm Service Agency, Notice LP-2165, "Suspension of MAL's and LDP's for Mohair," December 1, 2011, at http://www.fsa.usda.gov/Internet/FSA_Notice/ lp_2165.pdf; USDA Farm Service Agency, Notice LP-2175, "2013 Crop Year MAL's and LDP's," January 14, 2013, http://www.fsa.usda.gov/Internet/FSA_Notice/lp_2175.pdf; USDA Farm Service Agency, Notice LP-2188, "MAL and LDP Policy for Crop Year 2014," December 23, 2013, http://www.fsa.usda.gov/Internet/FSA_Notice/lp_2188.pdf.

[77] This section was written by Dennis A. Shields (7-9051, dshields@crs.loc.gov). For more information on crop insurance, see CRS Report R40532, *Federal Crop Insurance: Background.*

Agriculture Buildings and Facilities and Rental Payments account. Most of the remaining increase—as indicated in the Administration's request but not specifically mentioned in either the House- or Senate-reported bill—would represent additional funding for RMA's ability to improve program compliance, including efforts to reduce improper payments.

For the Federal Crop Insurance Fund mandatory appropriation, the FY2015 House-reported and Senate-reported bills concur with the Administration request for $8.7 billion, down 9% from the estimated level in FY2014. (The actual amount required to cover program losses and other subsidies is subject to change based on actual crop losses and farmer participation rates in the program.) The year-over-year decline is driven by expected lower commodity prices, which results in a reduced level of premium subsidies. The estimate also incorporates expected funds needed in FY2015 for crop insurance changes made by the 2014 farm bill, including additional coverage provided by the Supplemental Coverage Option (SCO) and the Stacked Income Protection Plan (STAX) for upland cotton.

Conservation[78]

USDA administers a number of agricultural conservation programs that assist private landowners with natural resource concerns. These include working land programs, land retirement and easement programs, watershed programs, technical assistance, and other programs. The two lead agricultural conservation agencies within USDA are the Natural Resources Conservation Service (NRCS), which provides technical assistance and administers most programs, and the Farm Service Agency (FSA), which administers the largest program, the Conservation Reserve Program (CRP).

The majority of conservation program funding is mandatory, funded through the Commodity Credit Corporation (CCC), and authorized in omnibus farm bills (about $5.5 billion of CCC funds in FY2015). Other conservation programs, mostly technical assistance, are discretionary and funded through annual appropriations (about $850 million in the FY2015 appropriations bills).

As discussed in more detail below, the Senate-reported bill accepts all of the Administration's proposed reductions to mandatory conservation programs, while the House-reported bill includes additional reductions. Both the House- and Senate-reported bills provide more than the Administration's request for discretionary programs.

Discretionary Conservation Programs

All of the discretionary conservation programs are administered by NRCS. The largest discretionary conservation program that funds most all NRCS operations is the Conservation Operations (CO) account. Both the Administration's request and the Senate conference report (S.Rept. 113-164), propose decentralizing General Services Administrations (GSA) rental payments and Department of Homeland Security (DHS) security services payments previously funded through the USDA Agriculture Buildings and Facilities and Rental Payments account. This amount is included in the total CO funding level for FY2015. The House-report does not specifically mention rental expenses in the conservation section, but funding levels appear consistent with this known change to paying for rent. After accounting for the GSA and DHS

---

[78] This section was written by Megan Stubbs (7-8707, mstubbs@crs.loc.gov).

payments, the House- and Senate-report bills increase funding for CO above FY2014 levels, while the Administration's request is actually a decrease from FY2014.

Both H.R. 4800 and S. 2389, as reported, further direct CO funding for a number of existing conservation programs (see **Table 8**). The committee reports (H.Rept. 113-468 and S.Rept. 113-164) include a number of congressionally directed actions for NRCS, including program administration, invasive species needs, wetland mitigation requirements, herbicide resistance actions, conservation practices and standard direction, species protection, and partner agreements. While these actions do not include a specific funding level, they can ultimately direct funding to congressionally identified projects, similar to earmarks.

Table 8. Conservation Operations Funding

(budget authority in millions of dollars)

Program	FY2014	FY2015		
	P.L. 113-76	Admin. Request	House report	Senate report
Conservation Operations[a]	813	815	843	849
Conservation Technical Assistance	711	717	747	0
Soil Survey	80	80	78	0
Snow Survey	9.3	8.9	9.1	0
Plant Material Center	9.4	9.2	9.2	0
Watershed Projects (Watershed Operations)	3.0	0	0	5.6
Conservation Delivery Streamlining Initiative	0	3.7	1.5	0

Source: CRS from H.R. 4800, S. 2389, H.Rept. 113-468, and S.Rept. 113-164.

Notes: The lack of a specified funding level does not necessarily indicate a Committee's lack of support for a particular sub-program, only that the bill and report language did not specify an amount for FY2015.

a. Total CO includes GSA and DHS rental payments of $28.6 million in the Administration's request and Senate-reported bill. The House-reported bill does not include similar language, but funding levels are consistent with these payments inclusion.

The Administration proposes renaming the Conservation Operations account as "Private Lands Conservation Operations" and consolidating the technical assistance funding for the mandatory conservation programs with CO. Neither the House- nor Senate-reported bills adopted this proposed change.

Funding also is provided in the House-reported bill (and in the enacted FY2014 appropriation and the 2014 farm bill) for the Watershed Rehabilitation program, which rehabilitates aging dams previously built by USDA.[79] The Administration proposed terminating this program contending that the maintenance, repair, and operation of dams are the responsibility of the local project sponsor. The enacted FY2014 appropriation included $12 million for the program and the 2014

---

[79] For additional information, see CRS Report RL30478, *Federally Supported Water Supply and Wastewater Treatment Programs.*

farm bill (P.L. 113-79) added an additional $250 million in mandatory funding for FY2014.[80] H.R. 4800 provides $25 million for FY2015 and S. 2389 includes no funding for the program.

Mandatory Conservation Programs

Mandatory conservation programs generally are authorized in omnibus farm bills and receive funding from the CCC, thus not requiring an annual appropriation. But Congress has reduced mandatory conservation programs through changes in mandatory program spending (CHIMPS) in the annual agricultural appropriations law every year since FY2003. Because money is fungible, the savings from these reductions are not necessarily applied toward other conservation activities. Prior to the 2008 farm bill, reductions to conservation programs through appropriations law peaked in FY2006 with a reduction totaling $638 million. Following the 2008 farm bill, reductions peaked again in FY2012, with total conservation CHIMPS of $929 million. The 2014 farm bill reauthorized, consolidated, and created a number of conservation programs that receive mandatory funding (over $5 billion in FY2015). The House- and Senate-reported bills would continue the CHIMPS to farm bill conservation programs of $206 million and $278 million, respectively.

The Administration's request has historically included annual proposed reductions to conservation funding, usually more substantial than Congress has supported. Both the Administration's request and Senate-reported bill reduce mandatory conservation program spending (CHIMPS) by $278 million in FY2015, while the House-reported reduction is slightly less at $206 million.[81] Sequestration is expected to reduce these programs further in FY2015, resulting in a total reduction to CHIMPed conservation programs of $396 million in H.R. 4800 and $403 million in S. 2389.

The number of conservation programs reduced through appropriations varies from year-to-year, however some programs are continuously reduced, while others almost never receive a reduction. Programs such as the Environmental Quality Incentives Program (EQIP) have been reduced annually since FY2003, while others, such as the Conservation Reserve Program (CRP) have not been reduced in over a decade. In FY2015, the Administration's request and Senate-reported bill include the same level of reductions, including allowing EQIP no more than $1.35 billion (authorized at $1.6 billion) and no funding for the Watershed Rehabilitation Program (authorized at $153 million[82]). The House-reported bill allows more for these two programs: $1.391 billion for EQIP and $92 million from the Watershed Rehabilitation Program. However, H.R. 4800 also

---

[80] Mandatory funding for the program was restricted in the FY2014 appropriation, but because the 2014 farm bill was enacted after the enactment of the FY2014 appropriation, the CHIMPS in appropriations did not apply to the new funding; therefore NRCS received the full $250 million from the farm bill for the Watershed Rehabilitation Program. According to NRCS, the agency will be able to obligate all of the new funding and still have a backlog of requested funding close to $336 million that will remain unfunded.

[81] For discussion purposes, since the Senate bill and Administration's request would reduce these programs to the same level, this paragraph refers to them having the same $278 million conservation CHIMP total. However, CBO was not consistent and gave the Administration credit for a level of CHIMPS that was not available to the Senate because of sequestration. Therefore the Administration actually is credited in **Table 13** with $403 million from two conservation program CHIMPS. See the text box in the later section "Changes in Mandatory Program Spending (CHIMPS)."

[82] Mandatory funding for the program originally was provided in the 2002 farm bill to remain available until expended. Since that time, annual appropriations have restricted this no-year funding to generate annual savings. In FY2014, this restriction resulted in savings of $153 million and is expected to save $142 million if fully restricted again in FY2015. The $11 million difference is an estimated reduction from sequestration.

---

limits the new Agricultural Conservation Easement Program (ACEP) to $385 million ($425 million authorized) and the Conservation Stewardship Program (CSP) to $1.166 billion (authorized to enroll up to 10 million acres). The Senate-reported bill does not reduce these latter two programs.

For more information on reductions to mandatory conservation programs through appropriations, see CRS Report IF00036, *Reductions to Mandatory Agricultural Conservation Programs in Appropriations Law (In Focus)*.

Rural Development[83]

Three agencies are responsible for USDA's rural development mission area: the Rural Housing Service (RHS), the Rural Business-Cooperative Service (RBS), and the Rural Utilities Service (RUS). An Office of Community Development provides community development support through field offices. This mission area also administers Rural Economic Area Partnerships and the National Rural Development Partnership.

In the Appropriations committee tables, H.R. 4800 recommends a total of $2.44 billion in discretionary budget authority for rural development programs in FY2015, which is $38 million more than in FY2014 (+1.6%). The Senate bill (S. 2389) would provide $13 million more in budget authority than the House bill. Both bills support about $36 billion in total loan authority.

If the rescission to the Cushion of Credit account (-$158 million in the Senate bill and -$155 million in the House bill) is not incorporated in the rural development section but included with CHIMPS as in the CBO score, then the net budget authority for rural development would be $2.59 billion in the House bill and $2.61 billion in the Senate bill (**Table 9**).

Salaries and expenses within Rural Development are funded from a direct appropriation plus transfers from each of the mission agencies. The House bill recommends a combined salaries and expenses total of $678.2 million for FY2015, $21 million more than in FY2014. The Senate bill would provide $682.9 million, $4.7 million more than the House bill.

Rural Housing Service (RHS)

The House bill would provide $1.72 billion in budget authority for RHS programs (after transfers of salary and expenses), $30.7 million more than in FY2014 (+1.8%). This is $99.5 million more than requested, and about $3 million less than the Senate bill. The House measure would support a loan authorization level of $27.6 billion, about $155 million more than in FY2014. The Senate bill would support a loan authorization level of $27.4 billion.

The single-family housing loan program (Section 502 of the Housing Act of 1949) is the largest loan account, representing 90% of RHS's total loan authority. H.R. 4800 recommends $25.0 billion in loan authorization for Section 502 direct and guaranteed loans, and the Senate bill recommends $24.9 billion. Both the House and Senate bills recommend the same loan level for Section 502 loan guarantees ($24 billion), the same as FY2014 and the Administration's request.

---

[83] This section was written by Tadlock Cowan (7-7600, tcowan@crs.loc.gov).

Table 9. USDA Rural Development Appropriations
(budget authority in millions of dollars)

	FY2012 P.L. 112-55	FY2013 P.L. 113-6 post-sequ.	FY2014 P.L. 113-76	FY2015 Admin. Request	FY2015 House-reported	FY2015 Senate-reported	Change from FY2014 to House $	%	Change from House to Senate $	%
Summary										
Salaries and expenses (direct)	182.0	192.1	203.4	225.1	224.2	228.9	+20.8	+10.2%	+4.7	+2.1%
Transfers from RHS, RBCS, RUS	471.9	420.9	454.0	434.5	454.0	454.0	+0.0	+0.0%	+0.0	+0.0%
Subtotal, salaries and exp.	**653.9**	**613.0**	**657.4**	**659.6**	**678.2**	**682.9**	**+20.8**	**+3.2%**	**+4.7**	**+0.7%**
1. Rural Housing Service	1,090.3	1,031.1	1,279.6	1,228.6	1,310.4	1,307.0	+30.7	+2.4%	-3.4	-0.3%
2. Rural Business-Cooperative Service	109.3	114.2	130.2	139.2	99.6	111.7	-30.6	-23.5%	+12.2	+12.3%
3. Rural Utilities Service	551.0	520.8	501.6	357.6	501.8	504.4	+0.2	+0.0%	+2.6	+0.5%
Office of the Under Secretary	0.8	0.8	0.9	0.9	0.9	0.9	+0.0	+0.6%	+0.0	+0.0%
Total, Rural Development	**2,405.2**	**2,279.9**	**2,569.7**	**2,385.9**	**2,590.8**	**2,606.9**	**+21.1**	**+0.8%**	**+16.1**	**+0.6%**
Alternate total (including rescissions)[a]										
Less rescission of Cushion of Credit	-155.0	-180.0	-172.0	-155.0	-155.0	-158.0	+17.0	-9.9%	-3.0	+1.9%
Net, Rural Development (in comm. rept.)	**2,250.2**	**2,099.9**	**2,397.7**	**2,230.9**	**2,435.8**	**2,448.9**	**+38.1**	**+1.6%**	**+13.1**	**+0.5%**
1. Rural Housing Service										
Administrative expenses (transfer)	430.8	383.3	415.1	397.3	415.1	415.1	+0.0	+0.0%	+0.0	+0.0%
Single family direct loans (sec. 502)	42.6	50.2	24.5	26.6	76.9	66.4	+52.4	+214.2%	-10.5	-13.7%
Loan authority	900.0	840.1	900.0	360.0	1,042.3	900.0	+142.3	+15.8%	-142.3	-13.7%
Single family guaranteed loans: Loan authority[b]	24,000.0	24,000.0	24,000.0	24,000.0	24,000.0	24,000.0	+0.0	+0.0%	+0.0	+0.0%
Other RHIF programs[c]	37.6	29.3	22.8	29.5	29.4	29.5	+6.6	+29.0%	+0.1	+0.3%
Loan authority	240.3	241.7	248.6	243.6	248.4	248.6	-0.2	-0.1%	+0.2	+0.1%

| | FY2012 | FY2013 | FY2014 | FY2015 | | | Change from FY2014 to House | | Change from House to Senate | |
	P.L. 112-55	P.L. 113-6 post-sequ.	P.L. 113-76	Admin. Request	House-reported	Senate-reported	$	%	$	%
Subtotal, RHIF	**511.0**	**462.7**	**462.4**	**453.4**	**521.5**	**511.0**	**+59.1**	**+12.8%**	**-10.4**	**-2.0%**
Loan authority	*25,140.3*	*25,081.8*	*25,148.6*	*24,603.6*	*25,290.6*	*25,148.6*	*+142.1*	*+0.6%*	*-142.1*	*-0.6%*
Other housing programs										
Rental assistance (sec. 521)	900.7	834.3	1,110.0	1,088.5	1,088.5	1,093.5	-21.5	-1.9%	+5.0	+0.5%
Other rental assistance^d	4.0	2.8	0.0	0.0	0.0	0.0	+0.0	0.0%	+0.0	0.0%
Multifamily housing revitalization	13.0	26.4	32.6	28.0	28.0	28.0	-4.6	-14.0%	+0.0	+0.0%
Mutual & self-help housing grants	30.0	27.7	25.0	10.0	30.0	25.0	+5.0	+20.0%	-5.0	-16.7%
Rural housing assistance grants	33.1	30.6	32.2	25.0	27.0	32.2	-5.2	-16.3%	+5.2	+19.4%
Rural Community Facilities Program										
Community Facilities: Grants	11.4	12.1	13.0	17.0	13.0	13.0	+0.0	+0.0%	+0.0	+0.0%
Loan authority	*1,300.0*	*2,200.0*	*2,200.0*	*2,200.0*	*2,200.0*	*2,200.0*	*+0.0*	*+0.0%*	*+0.0*	*+0.0%*
Community Facilities: Guarantees	5.0	3.6	3.8	0.0	3.5	3.6	-0.3	-7.3%	+0.1	+2.4%
Loan authority	*105.7*	*53.3*	*59.5*	*0.0*	*73.2*	*75.0*	*+13.7*	*+23.0%*	*+1.8*	*+2.4%*
Rural community dev. initiative	3.6	5.7	6.0	0.0	5.0	6.0	-1.0	-16.2%	+1.0	+19.3%
Economic impact initiative grants	5.9	5.5	5.8	0.0	5.0	5.8	-0.8	-13.5%	+0.8	+15.6%
Tribal college grants	3.4	3.1	4.0	4.0	4.0	4.0	+0.0	+0.0%	+0.0	+0.0%
Subtotal, Rural Comm. Facil.	**29.3**	**30.0**	**32.5**	**21.0**	**30.5**	**32.3**	**-2.0**	**-6.2%**	**+1.8**	**+6.0%**
Loan authority	*1,405.7*	*2,253.3*	*2,259.5*	*2,200.0*	*2,273.2*	*2,275.0*	*+13.7*	*+0.6%*	*+1.8*	*+0.1%*
Total, Rural Housing Service	**1,521.1**	**1,414.3**	**1,694.7**	**1,625.9**	**1,725.5**	**1,722.1**	**+30.7**	**+1.8%**	**-3.4**	**-0.2%**
Less transfer salaries & exp.	-430.8	-383.3	-415.1	-397.3	-415.1	-415.1	+0.0	+0.0%	+0.0	+0.0%
Rural Housing Service (programs)	**1,090.3**	**1,031.1**	**1,279.6**	**1,228.6**	**1,310.4**	**1,307.0**	**+30.7**	**+2.4%**	**-3.4**	**-0.3%**
Loan authority	*26,546.0*	*27,335.1*	*27,408.1*	*26,803.6*	*27,563.9*	*27,423.6*	*+155.8*	*+0.6%*	*-140.3*	*-0.5%*

	FY2012	FY2013	FY2014	FY2015			Change from FY2014 to House		Change from House to Senate	
	P.L. 112-55	P.L. 113-6 post-sequ.	P.L. 113-76	Admin. Request	House-reported	Senate-reported	$	%	$	%
2. Rural Business Cooperative Service										
Rural Business Program Account										
Guar. Bus. & Ind. (B&I) Loans	45.3	52.3	67.0	30.2	45.0	49.0	-22.0	-32.8%	+4.0	+8.8%
Loan authority	*812.6*	*890.2*	*958.1*	*590.8*	*880.6*	*958.1*	*-77.5*	*-8.1%*	*+77.5*	*+8.8%*
Rural bus. enterprise grants	24.3	22.6	24.3	0.0	20.0	0.0	-4.3	-17.8%	-20.0	-100.0%
Rural bus. opportunity grants	2.3	2.1	2.3	0.0	0.0	0.0	-2.3	-100.0%	+0.0	0.0%
Delta regional authority grants	2.9	2.8	3.0	0.0	0.0	3.0	-3.0	-100.0%	+3.0	0.0%
Rural business development				57.5	0.0	26.6	+0.0	0.0%	+26.6	0.0%
Rural Development Loan Fund Prog.										
Admin. expenses (transfer)	4.7	4.1	4.4	4.2	4.4	4.4	+0.0	+0.0%	+0.0	+0.0%
Loan subsidy	6.0	5.6	4.1	3.1	5.0	5.8	+0.9	+22.5%	+0.8	+16.4%
Loan authority	*17.7*	*17.4*	*18.9*	*10.0*	*16.2*	*18.9*	*-2.7*	*-14.1%*	*+2.7*	*+16.4%*
Rural Econ. Dev.: *Loan authority*	33.1	33.1	33.1	59.5	59.5	33.1	+26.4	+79.8%	-26.4	-44.4%
Rural coop. development grants	25.1	25.7	26.1	16.1	22.1	26.1	-4.0	-15.4%	+4.0	+18.1%
Loan subsidy	0.0	0.0	0.0	3.3	0.0	0.0	+0.0	0.0%	+0.0	0.0%
Loan authority	*0.0*	*0.0*	*0.0*	*25.7*	*0.0*	*0.0*	*+0.0*	*0.0%*	*+0.0*	*0.0%*
Rural Business Invest. Program: Grants				2.0	0.0	0.0	+0.0	0.0%	+0.0	0.0%
Loan subsidy				4.0	4.0	0.0	+4.0	0.0%	-4.0	-100.0%
Loan authority				*39.3*	*39.3*	*0.0*	*+39.3*	*0.0%*	*-39.3*	*-100.0%*
Rural Energy for America: Grants	1.7	0.0	0.0	5.0	0.0	0.0	+0.0	0.0%	+0.0	0.0%
Loan subsidy	1.7	3.1	3.5	5.0	3.5	1.4	+0.0	+0.0%	-2.2	-61.4%

	FY2012	FY2013	FY2014	FY2015			Change from FY2014 to House		Change from House to Senate	
	P.L. 112-55	P.L. 113-6 post-sequ.	P.L. 113-76	Admin. Request	House-reported	Senate-reported	$	%	$	%
Loan authority	6.5	13.1	12.8	47.3	33.1	12.8	+20.3	+159.3%	-20.3	-61.4%
Healthy Foods, Neighborhoods Initiative				13.0	0.0	0.0	+0.0	0.0%	+0.0	0.0%
Total, Rural Business-Coop. Service										
Budget authority	113.9	118.3	134.6	143.4	**104.0**	**116.2**	**-30.6**	**-22.7%**	**+12.2**	**+11.7%**
Less transfer salaries & exp.	-4.7	-4.1	-4.4	-4.2	-4.4	-4.4	+0.0	+0.0%	+0.0	+0.0%
Rural Bus.-Coop. Svc. (programs)	109.3	114.2	130.2	139.2	**99.6**	**111.7**	**-30.6**	**-23.5%**	**+12.2**	**+12.3%**
Loan authority	869.8	953.7	1,022.8	772.5	1,028.7	1,022.8	+5.8	+0.6%	-5.8	-0.6%
Alternate total (including rescission)[a]										
Budget authority	113.9	118.3	134.6	143.4	104.0	116.2	-30.6	-22.7%	+12.2	+11.7%
Less rescission of Cushion of Credit	-155.0	-180.0	-172.0	-155.0	-155.0	-158.0	+17.0	-9.9%	-3.0	+1.9%
Net, Rural Bus.-Coop. Svc. (cmte. reports)	**-41.1**	**-61.7**	**-37.4**	**-11.6**	**-51.0**	**-41.8**	**-13.6**	**+36.4%**	**+9.2**	**-18.0%**
3. Rural Utilities Service										
Rural Water and Waste Disposal Prog.										
Loan subsidy and grants	513.0	484.5	462.4	304.0	466.9	463.2	+4.5	+1.0%	-3.7	-0.8%
Direct loan authority	730.7	923.7	1,200.0	1,200.0	1,200.0	1,200.0	+0.0	+0.0%	+0.0	+0.0%
P.L. 83-566 loans	0.0	40.0	40.0	0.0	0.0	0.0	-40.0	-100.0%	+0.0	+0.0%
Guaranteed loan authority	62.9	56.6	50.0	0.0	84.7	50.0	+34.7	+69.5%	-34.7	-41.0%
Rural Electric and Telecomm. Loans										
Admin. expenses (transfer)	36.4	33.5	34.5	33.0	34.5	34.5	+0.0	+0.0%	+0.0	+0.0%
Telecommunication loan authority	690.0	690.0	690.0	345.0	690.0	690.0	+0.0	+0.0%	+0.0	+0.0%
Guar. underwriting loan subsidy	0.6	0.0	0.0	0.0	0.0	0.0	+0.0	+0.0%	+0.0	+0.0%

	FY2012	FY2013	FY2014	FY2015			Change from FY2014 to House		Change from House to Senate	
	P.L. 112-55	P.L. 113-6 post-sequ.	P.L. 113-76	Admin. Request	House-reported	Senate-reported	$	%	$	%
Electricity loan authority	*7,024.3*	*7,100.0*	*5,500.0*	*5,000.0*	*5,500.0*	*5,500.0*	*+0.0*	*+0.0%*	*+0.0*	*+0.0%*
Distance Learning, Telemedicine, Broadband										
Distance learning & telemedicine	21.0	23.1	24.3	25.0	20.0	24.3	-4.3	-17.8%	+4.3	+21.6%
Broadband: Grants	10.4	9.6	10.4	20.4	10.4	10.4	+0.0	+0.0%	+0.0	+0.0%
Broadband: Direct loan subsidy	6.0	3.7	4.5	8.3	4.5	6.4	+0.0	+0.0%	+1.9	+43.0%
Direct loan authority	*169.0*	*39.1*	*34.5*	*44.2*	*24.1*	*34.4*	*-10.4*	*-30.2%*	*+10.4*	*+43.0%*
Subtotal, Rural Utilities Service										
Budget authority	**587.3**	**554.3**	**536.0**	**390.6**	**536.2**	**538.8**	**+0.2**	**+0.0%**	**+2.6**	**+0.5%**
Less transfer salaries & exp.	-36.4	-33.5	-34.5	-33.0	-34.5	-34.5	+0.0	+0.0%	+0.0	+0.0%
Total, Rural Utilities Service	**551.0**	**520.8**	**501.6**	**357.6**	**501.8**	**504.4**	**+0.2**	**+0.0%**	**+2.6**	**+0.5%**
Loan authority	*8,676.9*	*8,849.4*	*7,514.5*	*6,589.2*	*7,498.8*	*7,474.4*	*-15.7*	*-0.2%*	*-24.4*	*-0.3%*

Source: CRS, compiled from tables in the joint explanatory statements or committee reports for S. 2389, H.R. 4800, P.L. 113-76, and P.L. 112-55. Post-sequestration amounts for FY2013 are from the USDA FY2013 Operating Plan.

Notes: *Loan authority* is the amount of loans that can be made and is not added to budget authority in the totals.

a. Amounts for the Rural Business Cooperative Service in this report are before the rescission from the Cushion of Credit account. This allows the agency total to remain positive. Appropriations Committee report tables show the rescission in the agency section, causing the agency total to be less than zero. This CRS report includes the Cushion of Credit rescission in the General Provisions section with changes in mandatory spending, as it is scored by CBO (**Table 13**).

b. This program became self-funding after enactment of higher loan guarantee fees being charged to banks.

c. Includes Section 504 housing repair, Section 515 rental housing, Section 524 site loans, Section 518 multi-family housing guarantees, single and multi-family housing credit sales, Section 523 self-help housing land development, and farm labor housing.

d. Section 502(c)(5)(D) eligible households, Section 515 new construction, and farm labor housing new construction.

The House bill would provide $1 billion in loan authorization ($142 million more than FY2014) for direct 502 loans, and $682 million more than the request. The Senate bill recommends $900 million in loan authority for the 502 direct loan program. The Section 502 loan guarantee program is self-funding, and needs no supporting budget authority. The Section 502 direct loan program requires a subsidy. The House bill recommends $76.9 million in budget authority to support a $1 billion loan authorization, $52.4 million more than in FY2014. The Senate bill would provide $66.4 million to support its $900 million loan authorization, about $40 million more than in FY2014.

H.R. 4800 recommends $3.7 million in budget authority to support $26.4 million in loans for the Section 504 Very Low-Income Housing Repair loan program. This is approximately the same loan authorization level as FY2014 ($26.3 million) and about $1.5 million less in budget authority than for FY2014 ($2.2 million). The Senate bill would provide the same in budget authority and approximately the same in loan authorization ($26.3 million). The Administration requested no funding for the Section 504 program. For the Multi-Family Housing loan guarantee program (Section 538), both House and Senate bills recommend loan authority of $150 million for FY2015, the same as for FY2014. Both House and Senate bills would provide about $28 million in loan authority for the Section 515 Rental Housing Program, and $9.8 million in subsidies. This is the same loan authorization level for the program in FY2014, but $3.2 million more in budget authority (+47.4%).

The Rental Assistance Program grants (Section 521) is the largest budget authority line item in RHS, accounting for 63% of the total RHS budget authority appropriation for FY2015. H.R. 4800 recommends $1.09 billion in new budget authority, the same as the request and a decrease of $21.5 million from FY2014 (-1.9%). The Senate bill would provide $5.0 million more than the House bill.

For Mutual and Self-Help Housing Grants, H.R. 4800 recommends $30 million, which is $5 million more than FY2014 and $5 million more than the Senate bill. For Rural Housing Assistance grants, H.R. 4800 would provide $27.0 million, 16.2% less than FY2014. The Senate bill recommends $32.2 million for the program, the same as for FY2014.

The Rural Housing Service also administers the Rural Community Facilities program. The program provides direct loans, loan guarantees, and grants for "essential community facilities" in rural areas with less than 20,000 in population. H.R. 4800 recommends a total of $30.5 million in new budget authority for the program to support a loan authorization level of $2.27 billion and $13 million in grants. This budget authority is $2.0 million less than for FY2014 (-6.2%). The Community Facilities account also contains appropriations for the Rural Community Development Initiative ($5 million in the House bill; $6 million in the Senate bill), Economic Impact Initiative grants ($5 million in the House; $5.8 million in the Senate), and Tribal College grants ($4 million in both bills). The Senate amounts are the same as FY2014; the House amounts represent reductions.

Rural Business-Cooperative Service (RBS)

The House-reported bill recommends $104.0 million in FY2015 budget authority to the RBS before the Cushion of Credit rescission and transfers of salaries and expenses. This is about $31 million less than in the enacted FY2014 amount (-23%). The Senate-reported bill recommends $116.2 million, which is 11.7% more than the House bill, but still less than FY2014.

If the Cushion of Credit rescission is incorporated (-$155 million in the House bill; -$158 million in the Senate bill), the net RBS budget authority accounted for in Appropriations committee tables is -$51.0 million in the House-reported bill and -$41.8 million in the Senate-reported bill.

Both bills would provide about $1.02 billion in loan authority for the various RBS loan programs, about the same as FY2014.

For the Rural Business Program account, H.R. 4800 recommends $65.0 million in budget authority, $31.5 million less than FY2014 (-32.8%). The Senate bill would provide $78.5 million in new budget authority for the Rural Business Program account, $13 million more than the House bill. The Rural Business Program account includes the Business and Industry (B&I) Loan Guarantee program ($49 million Senate, $45 million House), the Rural Business Development Grant program ($26.5 million Senate, $20 million House), and the Delta Regional Authority grant program ($3.0 million Senate, $0 House).[84] The House bill would reduce by $22 million (32.8%) the B&I Loan Guarantee Program's budget authority over FY2014, and the Senate bill would reduce the subsidy by $18 million. Loan authority recommended by the Senate bill for the B&I is the same as for FY2014 ($958.1 million). The House bill would reduce the B&I loan authority by $77.5 million over FY2014 to $880.6 million.

H.R. 4800 recommends $5.0 million in budget authority to support $16.2 million in loans for the Intermediary Relending Program, also known as the Rural Development Loan Program. This loan level is $2.6 million less (-14.0%) in loan authority than FY2014 and about $1 million less in budget authority. The Senate bill recommends $5.8 million in budget authority to support $18.8 million in loans. For Rural Cooperative Development Grants, H.R. 4800 would provide a total of $22.0 million, 15.3% less than FY2014. The Senate bill recommends $26 million, the same as FY2014. This appropriation is divided among Cooperative Development Grants ($5.8 million in both the House and Senate bills), Appropriate Technology Transfer for Rural Areas ($2.5 million House, $2.2 million Senate), Value-Added Product Grants ($10.7 million House, $15 million Senate), and grants to assist minority producers ($3.0 million for both House and Senate bills).

For the Rural Energy for America Program (REAP), H.R. 4800 recommends $3.5 million ($33.1 million in loans, and no grants), and S. 2389 would provide $1.4 million ($12.8 million in loans, and no grants).

The Administration requested funding for two new business programs for FY2015: the Rural Business Investment Program ($6 million) and the Health Food Financing Initiative (HFFI) ($13 million). The former program was authorized in the 2002 farm bill (P.L. 107-171, Section 6029), but never implemented; the HFFI was authorized in the 2014 farm bill (P.L. 113-79, Section 4206). H.R. 4800 recommends $4 million to support $39.2 million in loans for the new Rural Business Investment Program. The Senate bill recommends $0 funding for the program. Neither House nor Senate bill recommends funding for the HFFI.

---

[84] The Business Development grants program combines the Rural Business Enterprise grants and the Rural Business Opportunity grants.

Rural Utilities Service (RUS)

H.R. 4800 recommends $536.2 million in new budget authority for the Rural Utilities Service before transferring salaries and expenses, essentially the same as FY2014. The Senate bill recommends a slight increase to $538.8 million. These are about $148 million more than the Administration requested.

Loan subsidies and grants under the Rural Water and Waste Disposal Program account represent the largest share of FY2015 recommended budget authority under RUS programs (approximately 87% of total RUS budget authority). The House bill recommends $466.9 million in budget authority, $4.5 million more than FY2014 and significantly more than the Administration requested. This appropriation would support $1.28 billion in direct and guaranteed loans, $5.2 million less than FY2014. The Senate bill recommends slightly less than the House: $463.2 million. Most of the differences between the bills are accounted for among the grant programs:

- Water/Waste Water grants ($359.9 million House, $345.5 million Senate)

- Solid Waste Management grants ($4.0 million for both House and Senate bills)

- Individual Well Water grants ($993,000 for both House and Senate bills)

- Water and Waste Water revolving fund ($1.0 million for both House and Senate)

- Circuit Rider program ($15.0 million House, $15.9 million Senate)

- Technical Assistance ($19 million for both House and Senate bills)

- Grants for Colonias and Alaska and Hawaii Natives ($66.5 million for both bills)

- High Energy Cost grants ($0 House, $10 million Senate).

Both House and Senate bills recommend $5.5 billion in electric loans, the same as FY2014, and $690 million in Treasury rate telecommunication loans, also the same as FY2014. Most of the recommended loan authority is for direct Federal Finance Bank electric loans ($5.0 billion). Both bills also recommend the transfer to USDA Rural Development of $34.5 million in budget authority for electric and telecommunication administrative expenses.

For the combined distance learning, telemedicine, and broadband account, the House bill recommends $34.8 million and the Senate recommends $41.1 million in budget authority. The FY2014 appropriation was $39.2 million.

- For Distance Learning/Telemedicine, H.R. 4800 recommends $20.0 million in grant support, $4.3 million less than FY2014 (-11%). The Senate bill recommends $24.3 million for the grants program, the same as FY2014.

- For rural broadband, H.R. 4800 recommends $10.4 million for grants and $4.5 million for direct loan subsidies, each the same as FY2014. The associated loan authority however would decrease by $10 million from FY2014 to $24.1 million. The Senate bill recommends the same $10.4 million for grants, and a higher $6.4 million for loan subsidies, which would support the same $34 million loan level as in FY2014. The Administration requested $20 million in grants, $8.3 million in loan subsidy, and $44 million in loan authority.

Domestic Food Assistance[85]

Domestic food assistance represents over two-thirds of USDA's budget. This funding is largely for open-ended appropriated mandatory programs; that is, funding that varies with participation and in some cases inflation. The biggest mandatory programs include the Supplemental Nutrition Assistance Program (SNAP, formerly the Food Stamp program) and the child nutrition programs (including the National School Lunch Program and School Breakfast Program).

The three main discretionary budget items are the Special Supplemental Nutrition Program for Women, Infants, and Children (WIC), the Commodity Supplemental Food Program (CSFP), and federal nutrition program administration. For background on the major programs discussed in this section, see CRS Report R42353, *Domestic Food Assistance: Summary of Programs.*

For FY2015, the House and Senate committees both recommend total funding levels of about $109.8 billion. The bills differ by approximately $22 million, largely the result of differences in the child nutrition programs account, discussed below. Other non-monetary differences exist between the bills' FNS report language and general provisions.

Table 10 displays FNS's enacted appropriations for FY2011 through FY2014, and it displays the President's request, House, and Senate proposals for FY2015.

SNAP and Other Programs under the Food and Nutrition Act

Appropriations under the Food and Nutrition Act (formerly the Food Stamp Act) support (1) SNAP (and related grants), (2) a Nutrition Assistance Block Grant for Puerto Rico and nutrition assistance block grants to American Samoa and the Commonwealth of the Northern Mariana Islands (all in lieu of the SNAP), (3) the cost of food commodities as well as administrative and distribution expenses under the Food Distribution Program on Indian Reservations (FDPIR), (4) the cost of commodities for The Emergency Food Assistance Program (TEFAP) (but not administrative/distribution expenses, which are covered under the Commodity Assistance Program budget account), and (5) Community Food Projects.

The FY2015 appropriations proposals would provide approximately $82.3 billion for programs under the Food and Nutrition Act. This funding amount is an $81 million increase (less than 1%) over the total amount provided in FY2014.[86] The proposals would appropriate $3 billion for the SNAP contingency reserve fund, equal to past appropriations but less than the $5 billion requested by the Administration. The Administration has requested fewer funds for SNAP benefits than in FY2014 due to a forecast of a slight decrease in participation.[87]

---

[85] This section was written by Randy Alison Aussenberg (7-8641, raussenberg@crs.loc.gov).

[86] As an appropriated, open-ended mandatory program, SNAP funding is not the same as SNAP spending. SNAP regularly receives annual appropriations that are greater than the amount that the program spends. Better measures for SNAP program spending are from USDA-FNS's costs data, available at http://www.fns.usda.gov/pd/SNAPmain htm.

[87] USDA-FNS FY2015 Congressional Budget Justification, page "32-82." It is also worth noting that SNAP benefit *spending* will decrease from FY2014 due in part to the October 31, 2013 sunset of the American Recovery and Reinvestment Act's benefit increase; however, these funds were preappropriated and did not require funding from annual appropriations bills. See CRS Report R43257, *Background on the Scheduled Reduction to Supplemental Nutrition Assistance Program (SNAP) Benefits*, by Randy Alison Aussenberg and Gene Falk.

Table 10. Domestic Food Assistance (USDA-FNS) Appropriations

(budget authority in millions of dollars)

Program	FY2011 P.L. 112-10	FY2012 P.L. 112-55	FY2013 P.L. 113-6 post-sequ.	FY2014 P.L. 113-76	FY2015 Admin. Request[a]	FY2015 House-reported	FY2015 Senate-reported	Change from FY2014 to House $	Change from FY2014 to House %	Change from House to Senate $	Change from House to Senate %
Child Nutrition Programs[b]											
Account Total[c] incl. transfers	**17,319.9**	**18,151.2**	**19,913.2**	**19,288.0**	**20,537.0**	**20,523.8**	**20,497.0**	**+1,235.8**	**+6%**	**-26.8**	**-0.1%**
National School Lunch Program	9,981.1	10,169.6	11,278.6	10,576.3	11,369.1	11,369.1	11,369.1	+792.8	+7%	+0.0	+0.0%
School Breakfast Program	3,094.0	3,313.8	3,659.3	3,728.6	3,905.0	3,905.0	3,905.0	+176.4	+5%	+0.0	+0.0%
Child and Adult Care Food Program (CACFP)	2,686.3	2,831.5	2,949.5	3,080.0	3,149.7	3,149.7	3,149.7	+69.7	+2%	+0.0	+0.0%
Special Milk Program	12.5	13.2	11.9	10.6	10.4	10.4	10.4	-0.2	-2%	+0.0	+0.0%
Summer Food Service Program	392.7	402.0	434.7	461.6	492.7	492.7	492.7	+31.1	+7%	+0.0	+0.0%
State Administrative Expenses	206.9	279.0	289.7	247.2	264.0	264.0	264.0	+16.8	+7%	+0.0	+0.0%
Commodity Procurement for Child Nutrition	907.9	1,075.7	1,646.7	1,078.7	1,200.0	1,200.0	1,200.0	+121.3	+11%	+0.0	+0.0%
School Meals Equipment & Breakfast Expansion Grants[d]	0.0	1.0	35.0	25.0	35.0	25.0	25.0	+0.0	+0%	+0.0	+0.0%
Summer EBT Demonstration	0.0	0.0	0.0	0.0	30.0	27.0	0	+27.0	na	-27.0	na
Special Supplemental Nutrition Program for Women, Infants, and Children (WIC)											
Account Total	**7,252.0**	**6,734.0**	**6,618.5**	**6,715.8**	**6,823.0**	**6,623.0[e]**	**6,623.0**	**-92.8**	**-1%**	**+0.0**	**+0.0%**
Supplemental Nutrition Assistance Program (SNAP)[b]											
Account Total[c]	**70,613.4[f]**	**80,401.7**	**77,285.4**	**82,169.9**	**84,256.4[g]**	**82,251.1**	**82,251.4**	**+81.2**	**+0%**	**+0.3**	**+0.0%**
SNAP benefits	61,001.0[h]	70,524.6[h]	67,313.1[h]	71,885.0[h]	71,503.4	71,503.4	n/a	-381.6	-1%	na	na
Contingency Reserve Fund	3,000.0[f]	3,000.0	3,000.0	3,000.0	5,000.0	3,000.0	3,000.0	+0.0	+0%	+0.0	+0.0%
Advance Appropriations for FY2016	0	0	0	0	21,064.1	0.0	0.0	+0.0	n/a	+0.0	+0.0%

Program	FY2011 P.L. 112-10	FY2012 P.L. 112-55	FY2013 P.L. 113-6 post-sequ.	FY2014 P.L. 113-76	FY2015 Admin. Request[a]	FY2015 House-reported	FY2015 Senate-reported	Change from FY2014 to House $	Change from FY2014 to House %	Change from House to Senate $	Change from House to Senate %
State Administrative Costs	3,618.0	3,742.0	3,866.5	3,999.0	4,119.0	4,119.0	n/a	+120.0	+3%	na	na
Employment and Training	387.9	397.1	415.9	426.4	447.2	447.2	n/a	+20.8	+5%	na	na
TEFAP Commodities	247.5	260.3	265.8	268.8	324.0	324.0	n/a	+55.2	+21%	na	na
Food Distribution on Indian Reservations	97.0	102.7	100.2	104.0	119.7	119.7	n/a	+15.7	+15%	na	na
Commonwealth of Northern Mariana Islands	12.1	13.1	12.1	12.1	12.2	12.2	n/a	+0.1	+1%	na	na
Puerto Rico and American Samoa	1,751.60	1,842.8	1,880.4	1,901.5	1,937.9	1,937.9	n/a	+36.4	+2%	na	na
Commodity Assistance Program											
Account Total[c]	**246.6**	**242.3**	**243.7**	**269.7**	**275.7**	**275.7**	**275.7**	**+6.0**	**+2%**	**+0.0**	**0.0%**
Commodity Supplemental Food Program	175.7	176.8	181.8	202.7	208.7	208.7	208.7	+6.0	+3%	+0.0	0.0%
WIC Farmers Market Nutrition Program	20	16.5	15.3	16.5	16.5	16.5	16.5	+0.0	+0%	+0.0	0.0%
TEFAP Administrative Costs	49.4	48.0	45.6	49.4	49.4	49.4	49.4	+0.0	+0%	+0.0	0.0%
Nutrition Program Administration											
Account Total	**147.5**	**138.5**	**132.6**	**141.3**	**155.0**	**150.8**	**155.0**	**+8.7**	**+7%**	**+1.4**	**+0.9%**
Domestic Food Assistance Total	**82,782.6**	**105,553.0**	**104,098.0**	**108,585.6**	**112,047.1**	**109,824.5**	**109,802.1**	**+1,239**	**+1%**	**-22.4**	**-0.0%**

Source: CRS, compiled from appropriations committee tables in the joint explanatory statements or committee reports for P.L. 113-76, H.R. 2410, S. 1244, P.L. 113-6, P.L. 112-55, P.L. 112-10. Post-sequestration amounts for FY2013 were obtained from the USDA FY2013 Operating Plan (at http://www.dm.usda.gov/foia/docs/USDA_Operating_Plan.pdf) and USDA Office of Budget and Program Analysis unpublished tables, July 2013.

a. The FY2015 Administration Request reflected in this column is from the USDA-FNS budget request submitted to Congress in March 2014.

b. For the USDA-FNS programs that are open-ended mandatory programs (e.g., SNAP and the Child Nutrition Programs), the programs do not necessarily have the authority to spend all of the funds that have been appropriated. For such programs' historical spending, see USDA-FNS expenditure data available on the agency website at http://www.fns.usda.gov/data-and-statistics.

c. "Account Total" does not equal the sum of the programs listed below. Programs listed below are a selection of the funding that makes up the account total.

d. In FY2012, the funds were appropriated only as School Breakfast Expansion grants. In FY2013, FY2014, and in FY2015 proposals, the grant purposes were consolidated into one appropriation with both School Breakfast Expansion and Meals Equipment purchases.

e. According to H.Rept. 113-468, p. 48, this appropriation level reflects USDA's revision of their estimate.

f. Committee and conference reports show conflicting information for FY2011's SNAP (or Food and Nutrition Act) Account Total. The FY2011 continuing resolution (P.L. 112-10) gave USDA-FNS indefinite authority for Food and Nutrition Act programs, allowing for "amounts necessary to maintain current program levels under current law." The amounts for SNAP in S.Rept. 112-73 match the funds apportioned by OMB to USDA-FNS, and this column reflects those numbers rather than the amount in the original request or the conference agreement table. However, all committee reports indicate that a contingency reserve fund of $3 billion was appropriated, whereas the agency did not interpret a contingency reserve fund.

g. This is the Administration's request for FY2015 funding, but their request also included an advance appropriation for the first quarter of FY2016. The FY2016 amount requested was approximately $21.1 billion. Neither House nor Senate proposals include an advance appropriation.

h. Appropriations laws do not include the pre-appropriated funds provided by American Recovery and Reinvestment Act of 2009 (ARRA) for increasing SNAP benefits from April 2009 through October 31, 2013. See CRS Report R43257, *Background on the Scheduled Reduction to Supplemental Nutrition Assistance Program (SNAP) Benefits*.

Both the House and Senate committee reports include report language pertaining to the SNAP and Food and Nutrition Act programs account. The House's report includes language seeking updates on the impact of the Affordable Care Act on SNAP; directing FNS to enforce SNAP retailer regulations; and encouraging the implementation of certain provisions of the 2014 farm bill – wage and immigration verification, SNAP recruitment activities, and a feasibility study on the Commonwealth of the Northern Mariana Islands' transition to SNAP.[88] The Senate's report includes language encouraging the continued purchase of bison for FDPIR.[89]

Child Nutrition Programs

Appropriations under the child nutrition account fund a number of programs and activities covered by the Richard B. Russell National School Lunch Act and the Child Nutrition Act. These include the National School Lunch Program, School Breakfast Program, Child and Adult Care Food Program (CACFP), Summer Food Service program, Special Milk program, assistance for child-nutrition-related state administrative expenses (SAE), procurement of commodities for child nutrition programs (in addition to transfers from separate budget accounts within USDA), state-federal reviews of the integrity of school meal operations ("Coordinated Reviews"), "Team Nutrition" and food safety education initiatives to improve meal quality and safety in child nutrition programs, and support activities such as technical assistance to providers and studies/evaluations. (In addition, child nutrition efforts are supported by mandatory permanent appropriations and other funding sources discussed below in "Other Nutrition Funding Support.")

The FY2015 appropriations proposals would provide approximately $20.5 billion for child nutrition programs, 6% above the amount provided in FY2014. This total includes transfers from the Section 32 account.

For FY2015, the Administration requested funds for certain child nutrition discretionary grants. The House and Senate bills would provide amounts that differ from the request, and in one case, differ from each other:

- **School Meals Equipment and Breakfast Expansion grants.** In FY2014, the appropriations law provided $25 million for this purpose. For FY2015, the Administration requested $35 million. Both the House and Senate proposals would provide $25 million, $10 million below the Administration's request.

- **Summer EBT Demonstration Projects.** These programs provide food benefits to households with children over summer months, to make up for school meals that children miss when school is out of session and as an alternative to the Summer Food Service Program meals. These projects were last authorized and funded in the FY2010 appropriation (P.L. 111-80). The Administration requests $30 million to continue these projects in FY2015, citing the positive results of these demonstrations. The House Committee's proposal would provide $27 million; the Senate Committee's proposal does not fund this request.[90]

---

[88] H.Rept. 113-468, pages 45, 49-50.

[89] S.Rept. 113-164, page 70.

[90] See USDA-FNS Congressional Budget Justification, p. "32-24" for more details on this request. For the FY2010 funding and evaluation, see also USDA-FNS website, "Summer Electronic Benefit Transfer for Children (SEBTC)"http://www.fns.usda.gov/ops/summer-electronic-benefit-transfer-children-sebtc.

Child Nutrition Policies in General Provisions

The House and Senate proposals each contain general provisions that may impact the administration of programs funded by the Child Nutrition Programs account. In particular, both bills contain policies that would impact the implementation of the school meals nutrition guidelines.

Since the enactment of the 2010 reauthorization of the child nutrition and WIC programs (P.L. 111-296, "Healthy, Hunger-free Kids Act of 2010"), USDA-FNS has promulgated multiple regulations, formulated various program guidance, and published many other policy documents and reports. One of the major new rules to implement the law updates nutrition standards for the school meals programs.[91] Although the rule was finalized in January 2012, all aspects of the rule were not to be implemented immediately; for instance, some aspects of the new guidelines go into effect July 1, 2014, for the 2014-2015 school year. Three aspects of the new regulations that go into effect for 2014-2015 are: all grains served must be whole-grain-rich, new fruit requirements for breakfast, and the first of three weekly sodium targets ("Target 1").[92] On May 20, 2014, USDA-FNS announced flexibility on whole grain pasta, as response to feedback.[93]

Both the House and Senate committees' proposals include general provisions that would affect schools' implementation of these rules in school year 2014-2015. The House proposal (Section 739) would require USDA to issue waivers from the nutrition standards for 2014-2015 for school nutrition programs demonstrating a financial loss.[94] The Senate proposal (Section 747) would require scientific research before imposing sodium limits lower than "Target 1," a USDA report on the availability of whole grain products, and a USDA technical assistance plan to help schools meet nutrition guidelines.

The House proposal—but not the Senate proposal—also includes a policy rider (Sec. 742) seeking to prevent any processed chicken imported from China from being included in the child nutrition programs.

In addition to these general provisions, both the House and Senate committee reports include report language pertaining to the Child Nutrition Program account. The Senate report directs USDA to work with schools and industry to help implement the new whole grains requirements in the school meals programs and encourages FNS to work with national youth mentoring organizations to help administer the Summer Food Service Program.[95] The House report includes multiple instructions related to the implementation of the 2010 child nutrition reauthorization; it provides further details on the rationale and implementation of the bill's Section 739 (waivers from school meals' nutrition guidelines), encourages FNS to help states include cultural and regionally diverse foods in the school meals' programs, encourages FNS to work with

---

[91] The final rule for these guidelines was promulgated on January 26, 2012. For the rule and related resources, see USDA-FNS website at http://www.fns.usda.gov/school-meals/nutrition-standards-school-meals.

[92] See USDA-FNS Implementation Timeline, http://www.fns.usda.gov/sites/default/files/implementation_timeline.pdf, based on regulations.

[93] USDA-FNS, *Flexibility for Whole Grain-Rich Pasta in School Years 2014-2015 and 2015-2016*, Memo Code: SP 47-2014, May 20, 2014, http://www.fns.usda.gov/sites/default/files/SP47-2014os.pdf.

[94] A similar provision was included in the FY2014 appropriation law's *report language* "Joint Explanatory Statement." See CRS Report R43110, *Agriculture and Related Agencies: FY2014 and FY2013 (Post-Sequestration) Appropriations*, coordinated by Jim Monke, pages 62-63.

[95] S.Rept. 113-164, page 68.

---

stakeholders on the school nutrition personnel proposed rule, and directs USDA to submit a report as to whether USDA's cafeterias and vending machines meet the "Smart Snacks in Schools" standards.[96] The House report also directs USDA to give states additional flexibilities in conducting their monitoring and compliance reviews, and it directs USDA to implement the 2014 farm bill's fruit and vegetable pilot program at the beginning of school year 2014-2015.[97]

WIC Program

While SNAP and the child nutrition programs are appropriated mandatory programs, WIC is a discretionary program with the funding level entirely at Congress's discretion. Unlike the appropriated entitlements, an inadequate appropriation for the WIC program could reduce the number of pregnant and postpartum women, infants, and children served. It has been the practice of the appropriations committees to appropriate enough funds for WIC to serve all who are eligible.

House and Senate proposals would each provide $6.62 billion for WIC, a decrease of $93 million (1%) from FY2014 appropriations. The Senate proposal would restore the contingency reserve fund up to $150 million; but no additional reserve funding is provided by the House proposal. The FY2014 law restored the contingency reserve fund up to $125 million.

Both the House and Senate proposals include identical set-asides for WIC breastfeeding peer counselors and related activities ("not less than $60 million"), infrastructure ($14 million), and management information systems ($30 million). The House proposal also includes a $30 million set aside for transitioning WIC programs to electronic benefit transfer (EBT).

New WIC Program Policies in the General Provisions

The House and Senate proposals each contain general provisions that would impact the food eligible for purchase with WIC benefits, in particular, white potatoes.

USDA-FNS promulgated a WIC regulation, published as final in March 2014, that – among many other changes – prevents WIC benefit redemption for white potatoes.[98] WIC benefits, unlike cash assistance or SNAP benefits, are redeemable for particular foods tailored to whether a WIC participant is a woman who is pregnant, post-partum, or breastfeeding; an infant or child; as well as particular nutritional needs of the individual. The lists of foods are known as the "WIC Food Packages." States have some leeway to determine the specific foods that are eligible for WIC redemption in their state, but they must do so within federal regulatory requirements. Since 1973 (shortly after the program's establishment), the federal government has had regulations defining the WIC food packages. But before USDA embarked on the most recent process to update the food packages, they had not had a major revision since the 1970s. One of the changes in the new food package is the inclusion of a Fruit and Vegetable Voucher (FVV) for fresh fruits and

---

[96] For more information on these regulations, please see USDA-FNS website, http://www.fns.usda.gov/school-meals/regulations.

[97] H.Rept. 113-468, pages 45-47.

[98] USDA-FNS final rule and related resources available on agency website at http://www.fns.usda.gov/wic/final-rule-revisions-wic-food-packages.

vegetables. Based on recommendations made by the Institute of Medicine (IOM), the new food package does not allow participants to purchase white potatoes with their cash value voucher.[99]

The House proposal (Section 738) would bar USDA from excluding any vegetable (without added sugar, salt, fat) from the WIC "food package," presumably allowing white potatoes.

The Senate proposal (Section 745) includes vegetable language identical to the House proposal, presumably allowing white potatoes, but it also includes additional provisos. Namely, the Senate proposal would require USDA to conduct another review of the WIC food package, and, based on the results of that review, white potatoes (or other vegetables) would either continue to be included or would return to being excluded.

In addition to these general provisions, both House and Senate proposals' committee reports include report language pertaining to the WIC account. The Senate committee's report includes language on concerns with adhering to WIC income eligibility guidelines and the types of fish for the WIC "food package."[100] The House committee's report includes language seeking updates on the impact of the Affordable Care Act on WIC, directing FNS to issue an update on states' adherence to the income eligibility guidelines, and also directing FNS to monitor states' cost management efforts and to report on the sale of WIC benefits through social media.[101]

Commodity Assistance Program

Funding under the Commodity Assistance Program budget account supports several discretionary programs and activities: (1) the Commodity Supplemental Food Program (CSFP), (2) funding for TEFAP administrative and distribution costs, (3) the WIC Farmers Market Nutrition Program (FMNP), and (4) special Pacific Island assistance for nuclear-test-affected zones in the Pacific (the Marshall Islands) and in the case of natural disasters.

Both the House and Senate proposals would provide approximately $276 million for this account, an increase of $6 million (2%) from the FY2014 appropriation. The account's increase is due to CSFP; both bills would provide approximately $209 million for CSFP, an increase of $6 million (+3%) from CSFP's FY2014 funding level. All other programs in the account receive funding equal to the FY2014 appropriation.

Neither the House nor Senate proposals include related policies in the bill text, but both mention these programs in report language. The House report includes language expecting state agencies to consult with emergency feeding organizations on the need for converting entitlement commodity funds for handling and distribution costs.[102] The Senate report includes language encouraging USDA to work to provide funding for new CSFP states in future budget requests, directing USDA to expedite the obligation of WIC FMNP funds, and encouraging USDA to increase the supply of TEFAP foods through bonus and specialty crop purchases.[103]

---

[99] For further background on this issue, please see CRS Report IN10060, *Following the Debate on White Potatoes in the WIC Program*, by Randy Alison Aussenberg.

[100] S.Rept. 113-164, page 69.

[101] H.Rept. 113-468, pages 45, 48-49.

[102] H.Rept. 113-468, page 51.

[103] S.Rept. 113-164, page 72.

Nutrition Programs Administration

This budget account covers spending for federal administration of all the USDA domestic food assistance program areas noted above; special projects for improving the integrity and quality of these programs; and the Center for Nutrition Policy and Promotion (CNPP), which provides nutrition education and information to consumers (including various dietary guides).

The House proposal would provide about $151 million for Nutrition Programs Administration (+7% compared to FY2014). The Senate would provide $4 million more than the House.

Neither bill addresses policy issues in the bill text, but they do mention these programs in report language. The House report expresses concerns with formulation of the 2015 Dietary Guidelines for Americans.[104] The Senate report includes further details on using these funds to pay rent.[105]

Other Nutrition Funding Support

As in earlier years, domestic food assistance programs will receive FY2015 funds from sources other than appropriations:

- USDA provides commodity foods to the child nutrition programs using funds other than those in the Child Nutrition account. These purchases are financed through the use of permanent appropriations under Section 32.[106] For example, out of a total of about $1.1 billion in commodity support provided in FY2008, about $480 million worth came from outside the Child Nutrition account. Historically, about half the value of commodities distributed to child nutrition programs has come from the Section 32 account.

- The Fresh Fruit and Vegetable program offers fresh fruits and vegetables in selected elementary schools nationwide. It is financed with permanent, mandatory funding. The underlying law (Section 4304 of the 2008 farm bill) provides funds at the beginning of every school year (July). However, as in past years, general provisions in the House (Section 718) and Senate (Section 719) proposals would delay the availability of $122 million that is scheduled for July 2015 until October 2015. As a result, these proposals would allocate the total annual spending for the Fresh Fruit and Vegetable program mandated by the authorizing language by fiscal year rather than school year, with no reduction in overall support (savings scored in **Table 13**).

- The Food Service Management Institute (technical assistance to child nutrition providers) is funded through a permanent annual appropriation of $4 million.

- The Seniors Farmers' Market Nutrition program receives $21 million of mandatory funding per year (FY2002-FY2018) outside the regular appropriations process. See Section 4402 of the 2002 farm bill (P.L. 107-171) as amended by Section 4203 the 2014 farm bill (P.L. 113-79).

---

[104] H.Rept. 113-468, page 45, 51.

[105] S.Rept. 113-164, page 73.

[106] For more background on the Section 32 account, see CRS Report RL34081, *Farm and Food Support Under USDA's Section 32 Program.*

Agricultural Trade and Food Aid[107]

The Foreign Agricultural Service (FAS) administers overseas market promotion and export credit guarantee programs designed to improve the competitive position of U.S. agriculture in the world marketplace and to facilitate export sales. It shares responsibility with the U.S. Agency for International Development (USAID) to administer international food aid programs.[108]

Each year's agricultural appropriations measure provides more than three-quarters of the financial resources made available to FAS. Budget authority for other agricultural export and food aid programs is mandatory, and not subject to annual appropriations.[109] Funding for these mandatory programs is provided directly by the Commodity Credit Corporation under other statutes.

For FY2015, the Administration requested $1.777 billion for FAS/USAID programs that are funded on a discretionary basis (Title V: Foreign Assistance in **Table 2**). This is $61.5 million less than the FY2014 appropriation, with the reduction focused on the Food for Peace (P.L. 480) program. On the contrary, the House- and Senate reported bills have small increases over FY2014 ($1.856 billion and $1.843 billion, respectively), and do not reduce P.L. 480.

Foreign Agricultural Service

Both the House- and Senate-reported bills appropriate almost $183 million for the salaries and expenses of the Foreign Agricultural Service (FAS), almost $5 million (+2.7%) more than appropriated for FY2014. This appropriation funds FAS efforts to address trade policy issues on behalf of U.S. agricultural exporters, support trade promotion activities, and engage in institutional capacity building and food security activities in developing countries with promising market potential. The House-reported bill (H.R. 4800) adopted the Administration's proposed spending level ($182.6 million); the Senate-reported bill (S. 2389) increased the amount slightly.

Both bills appropriate to the FAS another $6.7 million to cover the salaries and expenses associated with implementing the export credit guarantee program. This is the largest export assistance program administered by FAS, and operates to facilitate the direct export of U.S. agricultural commodities and food products. Authorized by the 2014 farm bill at a $5.5 billion program level each year, this program guarantees the repayment of commercial loans extended by private banks in case a borrower defaults on making payments when due. There are no budgetary outlays associated with credit guarantees unless a default occurs.

House report language directs FAS to include performance goals in its future budget justifications for proposed changes to spending, and to present its budget submission in a way similar to that done by other USDA agencies to show the percentage of spending by major budget object class

---

[107] The agricultural trade section was written by Remy Jurenas (7-7281, rjurenas@crs.loc.gov) and the food aid section by Randy Schnepf (7-4277, rschnepf@crs.loc.gov).

[108] For background on USDA's international programs, see CRS Report R41072, *International Food Aid Programs: Background and Issues.*

[109] Mandatory funding for other agricultural export promotion and market development programs was reauthorized by the 2014 farm bill (P.L. 113-79) at slightly above $250 million each year. Annual funding levels are set at $200 million for the Market Access Program, $34.5 million for the Foreign Market Development Program, $9 million for the Technical Assistance for Specialty Crops Program, and $10 million for the Emerging Markets Program. Mandatory funding authorized for other foreign food aid programs under the 2014 farm bill will total about $250 million each year—all for the Food for Progress Program.

for each program and funding source. Senate report language recommends $1.5 million for the Borlaug Fellows Program to provide training for international scientists and policy makers from developing countries and $5.3 million for the Cochran Fellowship Program to provide short-term technical training for international participants in the United States. The Senate report also states appropriators' expectation that FAS fund the Foreign Market Development Cooperator Program and continue full mandatory funding for the Market Access Program (MAP) (see footnote 109). Senate appropriators expect FAS to administer MAP as authorized in law without changing the eligibility requirements for participation by cooperative organizations, small businesses, trade associations, and other entities.

Food for Peace Program (P.L. 480)

The Food for Peace Program includes four separate program areas, each with its own title: Title I—economic assistance and food security, Title II—emergency and private assistance programs, Title III—food for development, and Title V—the farmer-to-farmer program.[110] No funding for new Title I (long-term concessional credits) or Title III (food for development) activities has been requested since 2002, while the last Title I concessional commodity shipment occurred in 2006. Title V (farmer-to-farmer program) funding is mandatory in nature and linked to the overall pool of funding under the Food for Peace act—not less than the greater of $15 million or 0.6% of the amounts made available to carry out the Food for Peace Act during any fiscal year (FY2014-FY2018) shall be used to carry out the farmer-to-farmer program.

In contrast, the Food for Peace Title II program—which provides donations of U.S. commodities and cash to meet humanitarian and development needs abroad—relies on each year's agriculture appropriations measure for funding. Title II programs are both the largest and most active component of international agriculture food aid expenditures. Despite their funding origins in agricultural appropriations, Title II programs are administered by the U.S. Agency for International Development (USAID).

Food for Peace Title II funding has been embroiled in a long-running debate between the current (and previous) Administration and Congress over how Title II funds may be used. The Administration argues in favor of increasing the share of Title II funds available as either cash transfers, food vouchers, or for local and regional procurement of commodities in the proximity of the food crises in order to provide a more immediate (and lower-cost) response to international emergencies. In contrast, Congress favors using Title II funds to purchase U.S. commodities and ship them on U.S.-flag vessels to foreign countries with food deficiencies. Title II funding allocations are also affected by a provision in the 2014 farm bill (P.L. 113-79; §3012) which states that the minimum funding requirement for nonemergency food aid shall not be less than $350 million.

In FY2014, Food for Peace Title II humanitarian food aid was appropriated $1.469 billion. The Administration had requested to zero out the FY2014 Food for Peace Title II appropriations and shift all of the funding for food aid to the State Department's Foreign Operations Appropriations where it would be available as cash-based food assistance for emergencies; however, Congress rejected the Administration's request.

---

[110] Title IV of the Food for Peace Act involves general authorities and requirements.

The Administration's FY2015 budget request proposed that $1.4 billion be appropriated for Title II programs, of which 25% ($350 million) would be exempt from any U.S. purchase requirement and instead would be available as cash-based food assistance for emergencies. In addition, the Administration's budget request specified that $270 million of Title II funds be combined with an additional $80 million requested in the Development Assistance account under USAID's Community Development Fund and used to support development food assistance programs that address chronic food insecurity in areas of recurrent crises, thus achieving the required $350 million for nonemergency programs.

In contrast to the Administration, both the House-reported and Senate-reported appropriations bills would provide $1.469 billion, same as in FY2014, for Title II programs. The House bill also specifies that $375 million (not $350 million) shall be used for nonemergency programs, while the Senate bill specifies that $35 million be available under "enhanced" Title II section 202(e) program operations, including such activities as cash-based food assistance for emergencies.

Local and Regional Procurement (LRP) Projects

The 2008 farm bill authorized a total of $60 million of CCC funds (mandatory funds, not Title II appropriations) spread over four years for a pilot project to assess local and regional purchases of food aid for emergency relief. The 2014 farm bill changed the LRP pilot program into a permanent program with an authorization for discretionary funding of up to $80 million per fiscal year for each of FY2014-FY2018. However, neither the House-reported nor Senate-reported appropriations bill included any funding for the newly-authorized permanent LRP program. The Administration requested that 25% ($350 million) of Title II funds be available as cash-based food assistance for emergencies.

However, an amendment (H.Amdt. 856) to H.R. 4800 was adopted on the House floor on June 11, 2014, to provide $10 million for the LRP program, offset by a reduction to the Agricultural Marketing Service. Final action on the amended bill has yet to take place.

Two additional provisions affecting the Food for Peace program are included in the House bill, the first of which also appears in the Senate bill. As has been done in previous appropriations bills, Section 714 (of both H.R. 4800 and S. 2389) includes a provision that would limit, up to $20 million, the amount of Food for Peace funds available for reimbursement of the Commodity Credit Corporation for the release of commodities from the Bill Emerson Humanitarian Trust (7 U.S.C. 1736f-1). The second provision, provided in Section 727 (H.R. 4800), states that Title II funds "may only be used to provide assistance to recipient nations if adequate monitoring and controls, as determined by the Administrator of the U.S. Agency for International Development, are in place to ensure that emergency food aid is received by the intended beneficiaries in areas affected by food shortages and not diverted for unauthorized or inappropriate purpose."

McGovern-Dole Food for Education and Child Nutrition

The McGovern-Dole International Food for Education and Child Nutrition Program provides donations of U.S. agricultural products and financial and technical assistance for school feeding and maternal and child nutrition projects in developing countries. For FY2015, both the President's budget request and the Senate-reported level are in concurrence with recommended funding of $185.1 million—equal to the FY2014 level—whereas the House-reported bill includes a higher $198.1 million appropriation.

Note: Appropriations Provision on Industrial Hemp[111]

The production of industrial hemp in the United States is receiving appropriations attention. However, this provision is not part of the Agriculture appropriation, but is in the Commerce-Justice-Science (CJS) appropriations bill (both H.R. 4660 and S. 2437). Although hemp is an agricultural commodity used in a range of goods, hemp is a variety of Cannabis sativa and is of the same plant species as marijuana and subject to U.S. drug laws (see the **text box**).[112]

The House and Senate CJS provisions would block federal law enforcement authorities from interfering with state agencies, hemp growers, and agricultural research. Both the House and Senate CJS bills state that "none of the funds made available" to the U.S. Department of Justice (DOJ) and the Drug Enforcement Agency (DEA) "be used in contravention" of the 2014 farm bill. The House bill further provides that no funds be used to prevent a state from implementing its own state laws that "authorize the use, distribution, possession, or cultivation of industrial hemp" as defined in the 2014 farm bill (P.L. 113-79, §7606). In part this provision is in response to the seizure of 250 pounds of imported hemp seeds by federal authorities at Louisville International Airport in May 2014. The seeds were intended to be used by the state of Kentucky to plant industrial hemp in a pilot project authorized in the 2014 farm bill. Although the seeds were eventually released, the circumstances have resulted in uncertainty for hemp growers.[113]

Industrial Hemp: U.S. Laws and Policy

Industrial hemp is an agricultural commodity that is cultivated for use in the production of a range of hemp-based goods, including foods and beverages, cosmetics and personal care products, and nutritional supplements, as well as fabrics and textiles, yarns and spun fibers, paper, construction/insulation materials, and other manufactured goods.

Hemp, however, is a variety of Cannabis sativa and is of the same plant species as marijuana and is subject to U.S. drug laws. Under current U.S. drug policy all cannabis varieties, including hemp, are considered Schedule I controlled substances under the Controlled Substances Act (CSA, 21 U.S.C. §§801 et seq.; Title 21 CFR Part 1308.11). Despite these legitimate uses, hemp production and usage are controlled and regulated by the U.S. Drug Enforcement Administration (DEA). Strictly speaking, the CSA does not make growing hemp illegal; rather, it places strict controls on its production and enforces standards governing the security conditions under which the crop must be grown, making it illegal to grow without a DEA permit. Currently, cannabis varieties may be legitimately grown for research purposes only. No known active federal licenses allow for hemp cultivation at this time.

Until recently industrial hemp was not grown commercially in the United States. Changes to state laws in Colorado in November 2012 now allow for hemp cultivation in that state, which reported its first commercial hemp harvest in May 2013. Several Other states have passed laws that allow for growing hemp under certain conditions, including California, Hawaii, Indiana, Kentucky, Maine, Montana, Nebraska, New York, North Dakota, Oregon, Utah, Vermont, and West Virginia, with certain other allowances in other states. However, federal permitting requirements and other restrictions still apply and likely limit commercial cultivation and market expansion.

Given the absence of large-scale commercial industrial hemp production in the United States, the U.S. market is largely dependent on imports, both as finished hemp-containing products and as ingredients for processing.

The Agricultural Act of 2014 ("farm bill", P.L. 113-79, §7606) provides that certain research institutions and state departments of agriculture may grow industrial hemp, as part of an agricultural pilot program, if allowed under state laws where the institution or state department of agriculture is located. The farm bill also established a statutory definition of "industrial hemp" as "the plant Cannabis sativa L. and any part of such plant, whether growing or not, with a delta-9 tetrahydrocannabinol concentration of not more than 0.3 percent on a dry weight basis."

---

[111] This section was written by Renée Johnson (7-9588; rjohnson@crs.loc.gov).

[112] For more information, see CRS Report RL32725, *Hemp as an Agricultural Commodity*.

[113] Also see CRS Insight IN10087, *Congressional Efforts to Reduce Restrictions on Growing Industrial Hemp*.

Related Agencies

In addition to the USDA agencies mentioned above, the Agriculture appropriations subcommittees have jurisdiction over appropriations for two related agencies:

- The Food and Drug Administration (FDA) of the Department of Health and Human Services (HHS), and

- The Commodity Futures Trading Commission (CFTC)—in the House Agriculture Appropriations subcommittee only.

Agricultural Relationship to Related Agencies

The combined share of FDA and CFTC funding (Title VI) in the overall Agriculture and Related Agencies appropriations bill is about 13% of discretionary appropriations, or about 2% of the total.

These agencies are included in the Agriculture appropriations bill because of their historical connection to agricultural markets. However, the number and scope of non-agricultural issues has grown in recent decades. Some may argue that these agencies no longer belong in the Agriculture appropriations bill. Others say that despite the growing importance of non-agricultural issues, agriculture and food issues are still an important component of each agency. At FDA, food safety responsibilities that are shared between USDA and FDA have been in the media during recent years and have been the subject of legislation and hearings. At CFTC, volatility in agricultural commodity markets has been a subject of recent scrutiny at CFTC and in Congress.

Jurisdiction over CFTC appropriations is assigned differently in the House and Senate. Before FY2008, the Agriculture subcommittees in both the House and Senate had jurisdiction over CFTC funding. In FY2008, Senate jurisdiction moved to the Financial Services Appropriations Subcommittee. Placement in the enacted version now alternates each year. In even-numbered fiscal years, CFTC has resided in the Agriculture appropriations act. In odd-numbered fiscal years, CFTC has resided in the enacted Financial Services appropriations act.

Food and Drug Administration (FDA)[114]

The Food and Drug Administration (FDA) regulates the safety of foods and cosmetics; the safety and effectiveness of drugs, biologics (e.g., vaccines), and medical devices; and public health aspects of tobacco products.[115] Although FDA has been a part of the Department of Health and Human Services (HHS) since 1940, the Committee on Appropriations does not consider FDA within HHS under its Subcommittee on Labor, Health and Human Services, and Education, and Related Agencies. Jurisdiction over FDA's budget remains with the Subcommittee on Agriculture, Rural Development, Food and Drug Administration, and Related Agencies, reflecting FDA's beginnings as part of the Department of Agriculture.

FDA's program level, the amount that FDA can spend, is composed of direct appropriations (also referred to as budget authority) and user fees.[116] The President requested a *total program level* of

---

[114] This section was written by Susan Thaul (7-0562, sthaul@crs.loc.gov).

[115] Several CRS reports provide information on FDA authority and activities. See, for example, CRS Report R41983, *How FDA Approves Drugs and Regulates Their Safety and Effectiveness*, by Susan Thaul, and CRS Report R42130, *FDA Regulation of Medical Devices*, by Judith A. Johnson.

[116] Beginning with the Prescription Drug User Fee Act (PDUFA, P.L. 102-571) in 1992, Congress has authorized FDA to collect fees from industry sponsors of certain FDA-regulated products and to use the revenue to support statutorily defined activities, such as the review of product marketing applications.

$4.485 billion for FY2015, 2.3% more than the appropriated amount for FY2014.[117] The House-reported bill, H.R. 4800, puts the total at $4.485 billion and the Senate-reported bill, S. 2389, puts the total at $4.5 billion.

The President's request for FY2015 included $2.584 billion in *direct appropriations*, nearly 1% more than the FY2014 appropriation. The House bill would include $2.583 billion and the Senate bill would include $2.597 billion.

For *user fees*, the President requested $1.901 billion in fees to be collected through authorized programs to support specified agency activities regarding prescription drugs, medical devices, animal drugs, animal generic drugs, tobacco products, generic human drugs, biosimilars, mammography quality, color certification, export certification, food reinspection, food recall, and the voluntary qualified importer program.[118] In addition to the $1.901 billion in user fees from currently authorized programs, the President requested $260 million for as yet unauthorized fees for medical product reinspection, international courier, food establishment registration, food imports, cosmetics, and food contact notification. With those proposed fees, the President's total user fee request was $2.161 billion, bringing the total program level request to $4.745 billion. The House and Senate bills, as reported by the Committees, would provide the total fee amount requested for authorized programs ($1.901 billion) plus $1 million for fees authorized by this Congress related to the regulation of drug compounding[119] for a total of $1.902 billion.

Of the funds to be appropriated for FDA, the House-reported bill would make $20 million not available until FDA finalizes its January 2013 draft guidance on the evaluation and labeling of abuse-deterrent opioids (Section 734), and further directs that the $20 million go to FDA's Office of Criminal Investigation if FDA has not finalized the guidance by June 30, 2015.

In report language, the House committee notes that the recommended appropriations include the following increases: (1) $25 million for food safety activities; and (2) $12 million for pharmacy compounding activities. The committee also states its expectation that FDA fund the National Antimicrobial Response Monitoring System (NARMS) at $7.8 million, urging the agency to increase that funding "if warranted."

S. 2389, as reported, specifies that FDA use at least $150,000 to implement a labeling requirement concerning genetically engineered salmon. It also would require that $1.5 million of the budget authority provided for other activities (e.g., Office of the Commissioner) be transferred to the HHS Office of Inspector General for FDA oversight. In S.Rept. 113-164, the Committee notes that the recommended appropriations include the following increases: (1) $4 million for the

---

[117] The Consolidated Appropriations Act, 2014 (P.L. 113-76).

[118] Those who speak of FDA policy often use acronyms for the various user fee authorizing acts: Prescription Drug User Fee Act or Amendments (PDUFA), Medical Device User Fee Act or Amendments (MDUFA), Animal Drug User Fee Program (ADUFA), Animal Generic Drug User Fee Program (AGDUFA), Generic Drug User Fee Amendments (GDUFA), Biosimilar User Fee Act (BSUFA), and the Mammography Quality Standards Act (MQSA). Acronyms for others have not caught on: color certification, export certification, tobacco (from the Family Smoking Prevention and Tobacco Control Act), and food reinspection and food recall (both authorized by the FDA Food Safety Modernization Act (FMSA)). Several CRS reports describe FDA user fee programs. See, for example, CRS Report R42366, *Prescription Drug User Fee Act (PDUFA): 2012 Reauthorization as PDUFA V*, by Susan Thaul, and CRS Report R42508, *The FDA Medical Device User Fee Program*, by Judith A. Johnson.

[119] See Title I, the Compounding Quality Act, of P.L. 113-54, the Drug Quality and Security Act.

National Antimicrobial Resistance Monitoring System; (2) $4.82 million for counterfeit drug investigations; and (3) $11.7 million for cosmetics activities.

In addition to comments on specific amounts of funding, the House and Senate Committees on Appropriations lay out in the reports that accompanied their respectively reported bills (H.Rept. 113-468 and S.Rept. 113-164) their concerns with specific FDA activities. The reports include 60 statements that direct or encourage specific action.[120] The directions and encouragements covered most FDA programs, with the majority (37 out of 60) involving foods or human drugs. While directions and suggestions in the committee reports do not have statutory stature, they convey to the agency the concerns of committees that determine future appropriations. The topics the committees raise indicate both the broad range of responsibilities Congress has given FDA and a hint of the level of scientific expertise necessary to regulate items that touch many aspects of U.S. consumers' lives.[121]

Food safety activities at FDA are discussed earlier in this report in the section on "Food Safety."

Table 11 displays, by program area, the budget authority (direct appropriations), user fees, and total program levels for FDA in previous years: FY2012 (as calculated for the agency's June 2013 operating plan), FY2013 (as calculated by the June 2014 operating plan), and FY2014 (as calculated by the June 2014 operating plan). Regarding appropriations for FY2015, **Table 11** displays the President's FY2015 request, the House Committee on Appropriations-reported H.R. 4800, and the Senate Committee on Appropriations-reported S. 2389.

Consistent with the Administration and congressional committee formats, each program area in **Table 11** includes funding designated for the responsible FDA center (e.g., the Center for Drug Evaluation and Research or the Center for Food Safety and Applied Nutrition) and the portion of effort budgeted for the agency-wide Office of Regulatory Affairs to commit to that area. It also apportions user fee revenue across the program areas as indicated in the Administration's request (e.g., 90% of the animal drug user fee revenue is designated for the animal drugs and feeds program, with the rest going to the categories of headquarters and Office of the Commissioner, General Services Administration (GSA) rent, and other rent and rent-related activities).

---

[120] H.Rept. 113-468, submitted by Mr. Aderholt, from the Committee on Appropriations, to accompany H.R. 4800, Agriculture, Rural Development, Food and Drug Administration, and Related Agencies Appropriations Bill, 2015, June 4, 2014; and S.Rept. 113-164, submitted by Mr. Pryor, from the Committee on Appropriations, to accompany S. 2389, Agriculture, Rural Development, Food and Drug Administration, and Related Agencies Appropriations Bill, 2015, May 22, 2014.

[121] Topics addressed in the FY2015 committee reports, by program area, follow. *Foods:* Food Safety Modernization Act implementation (several items), food safety outreach and technical assistance, international regulation of lead in cosmetics, seafood advisory for pregnant women, seafood economic security, shellfish embargo, menu labeling, natural claims, regulation of tree nuts, and calorie display in vending machines. *Human drugs:* abuse deterrent drug development, compounding pharmacies, fixed dose combination drugs, global drug supply chain, prescription drug inserts, special protocol assessment agreement, sunscreen labeling and ingredient review, over-the-counter cold medicines for children, drug shortages, ANDA review prioritization, accelerated approval, Duchenne muscular dystrophy, generic drug labeling, opioid application approvals, and compassionate use. *Biologics:* bioethics committee, and blood plasma products. *Animal drugs and feeds:* use of medically important antibiotics for use in food animals, imported pet food product transparency, National Antimicrobial Response Monitoring System (NARMS), and veterinary feed directive regulation. *Devices and radiological products:* artificial pancreas, comprehensive device review assessment, mammography quality, and pediatric device grants. *Tobacco products:* deeming regulations regarding premium cigars, and tobacco product smuggling. *Toxicological research:* nanotechnology. *FDA-wide:* counterfeit products, import shipments, inclusion in clinical trials, user fee accounting, White Oak consolidation, and scientific integrity.

Table 11. Food and Drug Administration (FDA) Appropriations

(dollars in millions)

	FY2012	FY2013	FY2014	FY2015		
	P.L. 112-55	P.L. 113-6 post-sequ.	P.L. 113-76	Admin. request[a]	House-reported	Senate-reported
Foods	883	814	900	914	914	914
BA	866	797	883	903	913	903
Fees	17	17	17	10	10	10
Human drugs	979	1,187	1,289	1,335	1,326	1,340
BA	478	439	466	480	471	484
Fees	501	748	823	856	856	856
Biologics	329	308	338	343	344	343
BA	212	195	211	210	211	210
Fees	117	113	127	133	133	133
Animal drugs and feeds	166	155	173	172	172	176
BA	138	126	142	145	145	149
Fees	28	29	32	27	27	27
Devices and radiological health	376	384	428	437	440	437
BA	323	296	321	318	321	318
Fees	53	88	107	119	119	119
Tobacco products	455	459	501	532	532	532
Fees	455	459	501	532	532	532
Toxicological research	60	55	62	59	62	63
BA	60	55	62	59	62	63
Other (e.g., Commissioner Office)	223	251	275	279	279	279
BA	154	160	172	175	175	176
Fees	69	91	103	104	104	104
GSA rent	205	199	220	229	229	229
BA	161	150	162	169	169	169
Fees	45	49	58	60	60	60
Other rent, rent-related activities[b]	132	157	178	164	163	164
BA	106	118	133	116	116	116
Fees	26	40	46	48	48	48
Export & color certification (fees)	11	12	12	14	14	14
Priority review voucher (fees)	0	5	0	0	0	0
Food and drug safety[c] (BA)	—	46	0	0	0	0
Pharmacy compounding (fees)	—	—	—	—	1	1
Buildings & Facilities (BA)	9	5	9	9	9	9
Total Budget Authority	2,506	2,386	2,561	2,584	2,583	2,597
Total User Fees	1,326	1,645	1,826	1,901[d]	1,902[ef]	1,902[e]

	FY2012	FY2013	FY2014	FY2015		
	P.L. 112-55	P.L. 113-6 post-sequ.	P.L. 113-76	Admin. request[a]	House-reported	Senate-reported
Total, Program Level	3,832	4,031	4,387	4,485[d]	4,485	4,500

Sources: Funding amounts for FY2012 are taken from the FDA FY2013 Sequestration Operating Plan. The FY2013 and FY2014 amounts are from the FDA FY2014 Operating Plan, issued after enactment of the Consolidated Appropriations Act, 2014. FY2013 figures reflect sequestration. FY2015 request amounts are taken from the FY2015 congressional justification, issued in March 2014. Appropriations Committees reported amounts come from H.R. 4800, H.Rept. 113-468, S. 2389, and S.Rept. 113-164.

Notes: Consistent with the Administration and congressional committee formats, each program area includes funding designated for the responsible FDA center (e.g., the Center for Drug Evaluation and Research or the Center for Food Safety and Applied Nutrition) and the portion of effort budgeted for the agency-wide Office of Regulatory Affairs to commit to that area. It also apportions user fee revenue across the program areas as indicated in the Administration's request (e.g., 90% of the animal drug user fee revenue is designated for the animal drugs and feeds program, with the rest going to headquarters and Office of the Commissioner, GSA rent, and other rent and rent-related activities categories).

a. For user fees in the Administration's FY2015 request, this column shows only those that have been authorized. The request included an additional $260 million in proposed fees, allocated across several FDA program areas (foods $210 million; human drugs $0.5 million; animal drugs and feeds $18 million; devices and radiological health $4 million; headquarters and Office of the Commissioner $16 million; GSA rent $7 million; and other rent and rent-related activities $4 million).

b. Other rent and rent-related activities include White Oak consolidation.

c. The FY2013 Sequestration Operating Plan notes food safety and drug safety items that had not been included in the program-level appropriations.

d. The President's FY2015 request includes $1.901 billion in user fees from currently authorized programs (prescription drug, medical device, animal drug, animal generic drug, tobacco product, generic drug, biosimilars, mammography quality, color certification, export certification, food reinspection, and food recall) plus $260 million in proposed user fees (medical product reinspection, international courier, food establishment registration, food imports, cosmetics, and food contact notification) that would require authorizing legislation to implement. With those proposed fees, the President's total user fee request is $2.161 billion, yielding a total program level request of $4.745 billion.

e. The House and Senate committee-reported bills each included $1 million for fees related to pharmacy compounding that the President's request had not included. The President's request noted, "The Drug Quality and Security Act (P.L. 113-54) authorized three new FDA user fees: the outsourcing facility fees; the prescription drug wholesale distributer licensing and inspection; and the third-party logistics provider licensing and inspection fees. It is expected that collections for FY 2015 will be minimal."

f. In addition to mentioning other continuing and newly authorized fees, the House Committee-reported bill authorizes the crediting of fees (without indicating amounts) relating to outsourcing facilities, wholesale distributor licensing and inspection, and third-party logistics provider licensing and inspection as authorized by Title II, the Drug Supply Chain Security Act, of P.L. 113-54, the Drug Quality and Security Act.

Commodity Futures Trading Commission[122]

The Commodity Futures Trading Commission (CFTC) is the independent regulatory agency charged with oversight of derivatives markets. The CFTC's functions include oversight of trading on the futures exchanges, oversight of the swaps markets, registration and supervision of futures industry personnel, self-regulatory organizations and major participants in the swaps markets,

---

[122] This section was written by Rena S. Miller (7-0826, rsmiller@crs.loc.gov) and Jim Monke.

prevention of fraud and price manipulation, and investor protection. The Dodd-Frank Act (P.L. 111-203) brought the bulk of the previously-unregulated over-the-counter swaps markets under CFTC jurisdiction as well as the previously-regulated futures and options markets.[123]

The House-reported Agriculture appropriations bill would provide $217.6 million for CFTC in FY2015. This is $2.6 million more than FY2014 (+1.2%), but $62 million below the Administration's request.

The Senate Financial Services appropriations subcommittee, which has jurisdiction over CFTC appropriations, marked up a bill its bill on June 24, 2014.[124] The subcommittee mark would provide $280 million for CFTC, the same as the Administration's request. The Senate Appropriations full committee has not acted on subcommittee's recommendation.

Farm Credit Administration[125]

The Farm Credit Administration (FCA) is the federal regulator for the Farm Credit System (FCS). Neither the FCS nor the FCA receives a federal appropriation. The FCS is a borrower-owned lender operated as a government sponsored enterprise. The FCA is funded by assessments on the FCS entities that it regulates. As part of its congressional oversight, however, the Agriculture appropriations bill sets a limitation on administrative expenses (a maximum operating level) for the FCA—a check on the size of the FCA and the amount FCA can collect.

For FY2015, the FCA requested a $65.1 million limitation on expenses.[126] The Senate-reported bill concurs with the Administration's request. The House-reported bill would provide a level of $54 million, a level last seen in FY2010. The House committee report notes that FCA can exceed the limitation by 10% by notifying the Appropriations committees and that the $54 million level is the average level of obligations over the past five years. FCA's request notes a staffing replacement plan in which obligations for personnel are expected to rise about 20% in FY2014.[127]

Table 12. Farm Credit Administration Limitation on Expenses

(dollars in millions)

	FY2010	FY2011	FY2012	FY2013	FY2014	FY2015		
	P.L. 111-80	P.L. 112-10	P.L. 112-55	P.L. 113-6	P.L. 113-76	Admin. Request	House-report	Senate-report
FCA limitation on expenses	54.5	59.4	61.0	63.3	62.6	65.1	54.0	65.1

Source: CRS, compiled from tables in the joint explanatory statements or committee reports.

---

[123] A subset of the swaps market, called security-based swaps, which are swaps related to securities such as stocks and bonds, are overseen by the Securities and Exchange Commission (SEC).

[124] Senate Committee on Appropriations, "FY15 FSGG Subcommittee Reported Bill and Draft Report," at http://www.appropriations.senate.gov/news/fy15-fsgg-subcommittee-reported-bill-and-draft-report.

[125] This section was written by Jim Monke (7-9664, jmonke@crs.loc.gov).

[126] Farm Credit Administration, *Fiscal Year 2015 Proposed Budget and Performance Plan*, at http://fca.gov/Download/BudgetFY2015.pdf.

[127] Ibid, at p. 13, and p. 19.

General Provisions and Scorekeeping Adjustments[128]

The House- and Senate-reported FY2015 Agriculture appropriation bills each contain a total of about $1.2 billion in net offsets that effectively reduce the cost of appropriations in the rest of the bill. These reductions occur in Title VII (General Provisions) and in separate CBO scorekeeping adjustments. Reductions are made by limitations on mandatory farm bill programs (about -$800 million, **Table 13**), recessions from other appropriated accounts (-$13 million, **Table 14**), and other scorekeeping adjustments not usually detailed in the bills (-$410 million in the House-reported bill, -$510 million in the Senate-reported bill, **Table 16**). Some additional spending authorizations also may be made in General Provisions, including $143 million in the Senate proposal (**Table 15**).

Limitations and rescissions in appropriations are used to score budgetary savings that help the bill meet the discretionary budget allocation. By offsetting spending elsewhere in the bill, they help provide relatively more to (or help avoid deeper cuts to) regular discretionary accounts than might otherwise occur.[129]

The General Provisions title also contains many policy-related provisions that affect how the Executive branch carries out the appropriation or other authorizing laws. Some of these policy-related provisions are discussed earlier in this report in the sections relevant for each agency.

Changes in Mandatory Program Spending (CHIMPS)

For more than a decade, appropriators have placed limits on mandatory spending authorized in statutes such as the farm bill (**Table 13**). These limits are also known as CHIMPS, "changes in mandatory program spending." Mandatory programs usually are not part of the appropriations process since formulas and eligibility rules are set in multi-year authorizing laws (such as the 2014 farm bill). Funding usually is assumed to be available based on the statute and without appropriations action.[130]

When appropriators limit mandatory spending, they do not change the authorizing law. Rather, limits on mandatory programs come from appropriations language such as: "None of the funds appropriated or otherwise made available by this or any other Act shall be used to pay the salaries and expenses of personnel to carry out section [...] of Public Law [...] in excess of $[...]." Limits usually appear in Title VII, General Provisions, of the Agriculture appropriations bill.

---

[128] This section was written by Jim Monke (7-9664, jmonke@crs.loc.gov).

[129] For example, in FY2011, half of the $3.4 billion reduction in total discretionary appropriations between FY2010 and FY2011 was achieved by a $1.7 billion increase in the use of farm bill limitations and rescissions.

[130] This report uses the CBO compilation of CHIMPS, which in addition to limits on farm bill programs also includes the rescission from the Cushion of Credit account for the Rural Business and Cooperative Service (RBS). Including the Cushion of Credit rescission in CHIMPS allows the total appropriation for RBS to remain positive and concurs with CBO scoring. However, appropriations committee tables include the Cushion of Credit rescission in the RBS section, causing the net agency appropriations total to be less than zero (the alternative scoring method noted in **Table 9**).

Table 13. Changes in Mandatory Program Spending (CHIMPS)

(dollars in millions)

CHIMPS	FY2012 P.L. 112-55	FY2013 P.L. 113-6 post-sequ.	FY2014 P.L. 113-76	FY2015 Admin. Request	FY2015 House-reported	FY2015 Senate-reported
Farm Bill CHIMPS						
Environmental Quality Incentives Program	-350.0	-279.0	-272.0	-250.0	-95.0	-136.0
Watershed Rehabilitation Program	-165.0	-165.0	-153.0	-153.0	-50.0	-142.0
Wetlands Reserve Program	-200.0					
Conservation Stewardship Program	-76.5				-31.0	
Agric. Conservation Easement Program					-30.0	
Farmland Protection Program	-50.0					
Grasslands Reserve Program	-30.0					
Wildlife Habitat Incentive Program	-35.0	-9.0				
Voluntary Public Access Program	-17.0					
Agricultural Management Assistance	-5.0	-5.0				
Fresh Fruit and Vegetable Program[a]	-133.0	-117.0	-119.0	-122.0	-122.0	-122.0
SNAP employment and training[b]	-11.0					
Biorefinery Assistance Program			-40.7		-24.0	
Bioenergy Program for Advanced Biofuels	-40.0		-8.0			
Biomass Crop Assistance Program	-28.0				-10.0	
Rural Energy for America Program	-48.0				-16.0	
Repowering Assistance		-28.0				
Crop insurance good performance discount	-25.0					
Microenterpreneur Assistance Program	-3.0					
Subtotal, Farm Bill CHIMPS	**-1,216.5**	**-603.0**	**-592.7**	**-525.0**	**-378.0**	**-400.0**
Other CHIMPS (rescissions of mandatory accounts)						
Cushion of Credit (Rural Development)	-155.0	-180.0	-172.0	-155.0	-155.0	-158.0
Section 32	-150.0	-110.0	-189.0	-203.0	-121.0	-121.0
Emergency Livestock Assistance Program				-125.0	-125.0	-125.0
Export credit	-20.2					
Trade Adjustment Assistance for Farmers	-90.0					
Total CHIMPS	**-1,631.8**	**-893.0**	**-953.7**	**-1,008.0**	**-779.0**	**-804.0**

Source: CRS, based on categorization of CHIMPS in unpublished CBO tables and drawn from tables in the joint explanatory statements or committee reports for S. 2389, H.R. 4800, P.L. 113-6, P.L. 113-76, and P.L. 112-55.

a. Delays funding from July until October of the same calendar year, effectively allocating the authorization by fiscal year rather than school year—with no reduction in overall support—and savings being scored.

b. The 2002 and 2008 farm bills authorized $90 million in mandatory funding for SNAP E&T, which was limited by various laws. The FY2014 appropriation continued that reduced level. The enacted 2014 farm bill (P.L. 113-79) restored available E&T funding to $90 million.

Historically, expenditure decisions are assumed to rest with appropriations committees.[131] The division over who should fund certain agriculture programs—appropriators or authorizers—has roots dating to the 1930s. Variable outlays for the farm commodity programs were difficult to budget and resembled entitlements. Mandatory funding—the Commodity Credit Corporation (CCC)—was created to remove the unpredictable funding issue from the appropriations process.

The dynamic changed after the 1996 farm bill when mandatory funds were used for programs that usually were discretionary. Appropriators had not funded some programs as much as authorizers had desired, and authorizing committees wrote farm bills using the mandatory funding at their discretion. Tension arose over who should fund certain activities. Some question whether the CCC should be used for programs that are not variable. The programs affected by CHIMPS typically include conservation, rural development, bioenergy, and some smaller nutrition assistance programs. CHIMPS have not affected the farm commodity programs or the primary nutrition assistance programs (such as SNAP).

The House-reported bill contains $779 million of CHIMPS, and the Senate-reported bill $804 million of CHIMPS. Both of these amounts are smaller than the CHIMP levels that were enacted in FY2011-FY2014 (**Table 13**).

For more information on reductions to mandatory conservation programs through appropriations, see CRS Report IF00036, *Reductions to Mandatory Agricultural Conservation Programs in Appropriations Law (In Focus)*. For more background generally, see CRS Report R41245, *Reductions in Mandatory Agriculture Program Spending*.

Budget Sequestration and CHIMPS

A complicating factor in understanding the CHIMP amounts for FY2015 is a methodological difference in how CBO scored the Administration's request compared with the House and Senate bills. Budget sequestration of mandatory accounts occurred in FY2014 and FY2015, reducing the amount available to most mandatory programs regardless of whether reductions were made in appropriations. For example, the complete prohibition on spending for the Watershed Rehabilitation Program resulted in a smaller $153 million CHIMP in FY2014 than the $165 million CHIMP in FY2013, even though the same $165 million program authority was available initially (**Table 13**).

Sequestration was incorporated into the amounts available for each program *before* the CHIMPS were computed in FY2014 and FY2015—*except* for the accounting of the Administration's FY2015 request. By not incorporating sequestration in the FY2015 estimates of the Administration request, CBO gave the Administration more credit for some CHIMPS than the House or Senate bills. For example, the Administration and the Senate proposed the same level of proposed program activity for the Environmental Quality Incentives Program (EQIP) in FY2015, but each was credited a different CHIMP amount. The CBO score of the Administration's CHIMP of EQIP was $250 million, but the score of the Senate bill's CHIMP was $136 million (**Table 13**); the $114 million difference is the implied amount of sequestration on the $1.6 billion farm bill authorization. Similar calculations may be made for other programs in **Table 13**.

This difference is important, for example, in reconciling the $20.9 billion discretionary total of the House bill (and the FY2014 level) with the $20.4 billion total for the Administration's request (**Table 2**). While it may appear that the Administration was proposing an overall reduction in spending from the $20.9 billion level of FY2014 and less than the FY2015 House and Senate bills, some of the difference is because the Administration was given credit for larger CHIMPS than the House and Senate bills.

---

[131] Summarized from Galen Fountain, (former) Majority Clerk of the Senate Agriculture Appropriations Subcommittee, "Funding Rural Development Programs: Past, Present, and Future," p. 4, at the 2009 USDA Agricultural Outlook Forum, February 22, 2009, at http://www.usda.gov/oce/forum/2009_Speeches/Speeches/Fountain.pdf.

Rescissions

Rescissions are a method of permanently cancelling the availability of funds that were provided by a previous appropriations law, and in doing so achieving or scoring budgetary savings.[132]

As an offset, rescissions can allow more spending in an appropriations bill. But by cancelling an authorization, a rescission can prevent an unobligated budget authority from being reallocated or repurposed by future appropriations. Often rescissions relate to the unobligated balances of funds still available for a specific purpose that were appropriated a year or more ago (e.g., buildings and facilities funding that remains available until expended for specific projects, or disaster response funds for losses due to a specifically-named hurricane).

Rescissions in the FY2015 Administration request and in the House- and Senate-reported bills are small by comparison to recent years. For FY2015, the request and each chamber's bill would rescind $13 million, compared to a $33 million rescission in FY2014; **Table 14**). The FY2011 appropriation made unusually large rescissions (-$372 million) compared with prior and succeeding years and was difficult to repeat in the following years. Nonetheless, the FY2011 rescissions helped reduce the impact of that year's smaller total spending level because they offset relatively larger appropriations to agencies than would otherwise have been possible.

Table 14. Rescissions from (Prior-Year) Budget Authority

(dollars in millions)

Rescissions	FY2012 P.L. 112-55	FY2013 P.L. 113-6 post-sequ.	FY2014 P.L. 113-76	FY2015 Admin. Request	FY2015 House-reported	FY2015 Senate-reported
P.L. 480 Title I	-2.3			-13.0	-13.0	-13.0
Agriculture buildings and facilities			-30.0			
Rural Housing Service			-1.3			
Resource Conservation and Development			-2.0			
Broadband loan balances		-25.3				
NIFA buildings and facilities	-2.5					
Forestry incentives	-6.0					
Great Plains Conservation	-0.5					
Ocean freight	-3.2					
Office of Advocacy and Outreach	-4.0					
Foreign currency program	-0.3					
Total	**-18.9**	**-25.3**	**-33.3**	**-13.0**	**-13.0**	**-13.0**

Source: CRS, compiled from tables in the joint explanatory statements or committee reports for S. 2389, H.R. 4800, P.L. 113-6, P.L. 113-76, and P.L. 112-55.

---

[132] Rescissions to mandatory programs are counted in the CHIMPS section.

Other Appropriations (Including Emergency Disaster Programs)

The General Provisions title may contain appropriations for activities that are not part of regular agency appropriations. These sometimes include supplemental or disaster appropriations, and may be offset in scorekeeping adjustments by emergency spending designations.

Table 15 shows that for FY2015, the Senate-reported bill contains funding in Sec. 738 for several emergency conservation and emergency forestry activities, some of which are part of a $100 million emergency spending provision that does not apply to the spending limits.[133] The House bill and the Administration's request do not include these items.

Table 15. Other Appropriations in General Provisions

(budget authority in millions of dollars)

Other spending provisions	FY2012 P.L. 112-55	FY2013 P.L. 113-6 post-sequ.	FY2014 P.L. 113-76	FY2015 Admin. Request	FY2015 House-reported	FY2015 Senate-reported
Water Bank	7.5		4.0			4.0
Hardwood trees reforestation pilot	0.6	0.6	0.6			0.6
Geographically disadvantaged farmers	2.0	1.8	2.0			2.0
FDA salaries and expenses		46.2				
FDA user fees			79.0			
Citrus greening			20.0			
Hunger Commission			1.0			
SW Border Regional Commission				2.0		
Emergency Watershed Protection		60.5				25.0
Emergency Conservation Program		10.3				11.8
Emergency Forest Restoration		13.1				
Total (before disaster provisions)	**10.1**	**132.5**	**106.6**	**2.0**	**0.0**	**43.3**
Disaster provisions, subtotal	**367.0**					**100.0**
Emergency Watershed Protection	*215.9*					*85.0*
Emergency Conservation Program	*122.7*					
Emergency Forest Restoration	*28.4*					*15.0*
Total (including disaster funding)	**377.1**	**132.5**	**106.6**	**2.0**	**0.0**	**143.3**

Source: CRS, compiled from tables in the joint explanatory statements or committee reports for S. 2389, H.R. 4800, P.L. 113-6, P.L. 113-76, and P.L. 112-55.

---

[133] These are in addition to the "permanent agricultural disaster" programs for livestock and fruit trees authorized in the 2014 farm bill and funded with mandatory funds. See CRS Report RS21212, *Agricultural Disaster Assistance.*

Other Scorekeeping Adjustments

Scorekeeping adjustments are a final part of the accounting of the appropriations bill that is not necessarily shown in the tables published by the appropriations committees.[134] These adjustments are critical, however, for the bill to reach the desired total amount that complies with the 302(b) spending limit for the subcommittee. Some of these amounts are not necessarily specified by provisions in the bill, but are related to program operations. CBO calculates and reports these scorekeeping adjustments in unpublished tables.

For FY2015, the other scorekeeping adjustments in the House-reported bill total -$410 million, and in the Senate-reported bill total -$510 million (**Table 16**). The scorekeeping amounts in the House and Senate bills are the same, except for the Senate bill's $100 million disaster designation for two emergency conservation and emergency forestry programs.

Also, the regular FY2015 scorekeeping adjustments are about $200 million greater than in FY2014 and past years due to an increase in the magnitude of "negative subsidies" in several USDA loan programs. These negative subsidies effectively reflect "income" to the government when loan program operations cost less than appropriated though fees or better-than-expected loan repayment. These negative subsidies have become larger in recent years, and are helping to offset more of the appropriation.

Table 16. Scorekeeping Adjustments

(dollars in millions)

Other scorekeeping adjustments	FY2012 P.L. 112-55	FY2013 P.L. 113-6 post-seq.	FY2014 P.L. 113-76	FY2015 Admin. Request	FY2015 House-reported	FY2015 Senate-reported
Denali Commission (permanent)		4.0	4.0	4.0	-3.0	-3.0
Interest Native American Fund Endow.		5.0	5.0	5.0		
Child nutrition equipment grants		1.0	1.0	1.0	1.0	1.0
Loan program negative subsidies						
Rural housing negative subsidy	-7.0	-62.0	-62.0	-141.0	-141.0	-141.0
Rural community facilities negative subsidy	-4.0	-14.0	-41.0	-90.0	-90.0	-90.0
Rural elec. & tele. loan negative subsidy	-60.0	-60.0	-92.0	-152.0	-152.0	-152.0
Rural water & waste loan negative subsidy				-2.0	-2.0	-2.0
Agricultural credit loan negative subsidy	-1.0	-3.0	-6.0	-23.0	-23.0	-23.0
Subtotal, negative subsidies	**-72.0**	**-139.0**	**-201.0**	**-408.0**	**-408.0**	**-408.0**
Emergency designations, not in 302(b)	-367.0					-100.0
Total	**-439.0**	**-129.0**	**-191.0**	**-398.0**	**-410.0**	**-510.0**

Source: CRS, compiled from unpublished CBO tables.

---

[134] Although CHIMPS sometimes are considered to be scorekeeping adjustments and are shown in committee tables, they are discussed elsewhere in this report. This section discusses the unpublished, other scorekeeping adjustments.

Appendix. Historical Trends

This appendix offers historical perspective on trends in mandatory vs. discretionary spending, and a primary division of the appropriation into nutrition vs. other. It also shows inflation-adjusted amounts, and relationships to the size of the economy (GDP) and the federal budget. The enacted FY2014 appropriation in P.L. 113-76 is the basis for comparison throughout most of this section.

Discretionary Agriculture appropriations peaked in FY2010, although mandatory nutrition spending has continued to rise. In inflation-adjusted terms, the rise in mandatory spending and the total appropriation since FY2012 is small. See **Figure A-1** for the mandatory and discretionary breakdown; **Table A-1** contains the nominal data, and **Table A-2** contains the inflation-adjusted data. See **Table A-3** for the compounded annualized percentage changes over time periods.

- Over the past 10 years (since FY2004), total Agriculture appropriations have grown at an average annualized rate (compounded annual rate) of +5.3% per year (+3.0% on an inflation-adjusted basis).

- The mandatory spending portion of this total shows a +6.0% average annual increase over the past 10 years (+3.7% on an inflation-adjusted basis).

- The discretionary portion has an average annual 10-year increase of +2.2% (constant on an inflation-adjusted basis). In FY2004, 19% of the total agriculture appropriation was for discretionary; in FY2014, that ratio had decreased to 14% since mandatory spending rose faster than discretionary spending.

Figure A-1. Total Agriculture Appropriations: Mandatory and Discretionary

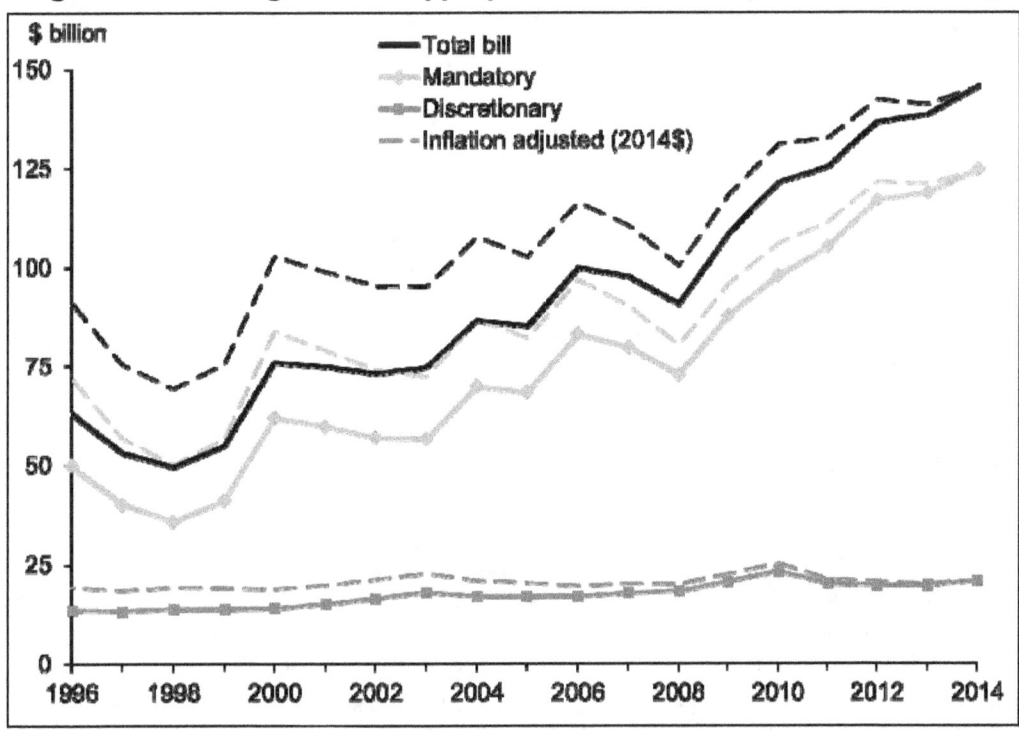

Source: CRS. Fiscal year budget authority. Inflation-adjusted amounts are based on the GDP price deflator.
Notes: Includes only regular annual appropriations for USDA (except the Forest Service), FDA, and CFTC (regardless of jurisdiction).

Another way to divide the total agriculture appropriation is domestic nutrition compared to everything else (**Figure A-2**). Domestic nutrition appropriations include primarily the child nutrition programs (school lunch and related programs), the Special Supplemental Nutrition Assistance Program (SNAP)—both of which are mandatory—and the Special Supplemental Nutrition Program for Women, Infants, and Children (WIC), which is discretionary. The "rest of the bill" includes other USDA programs (except the Forest Service), FDA and CFTC.

- The portion of the total for domestic nutrition programs has risen at an 8.7% average annual rate over 10 years (+6.3% on an inflation-adjusted basis). In FY2004, 55% of the total agriculture appropriation was for domestic nutrition. In FY2014, 75% of the total is for domestic nutrition.

- Most of the domestic nutrition program budget is mandatory spending, primarily in SNAP and the child nutrition programs. The mandatory spending portion rose at a +9.1% average annual rate over 10 years (+6.8% on an inflation-adjusted basis). By comparison, mandatory spending within the rest of the rest of the bill decreased at a -1.7% average annual rate over 10 years (-3.8% on an inflation-adjusted basis).

- The portion of the total for the rest of the bill (non-nutrition rest) has decreased at a -0.6% average annual rate over 10 years (-2.8% per year on an inflation-adjusted basis).

Figure A-2. Total Agriculture Appropriations: Domestic Nutrition and Rest of Bill

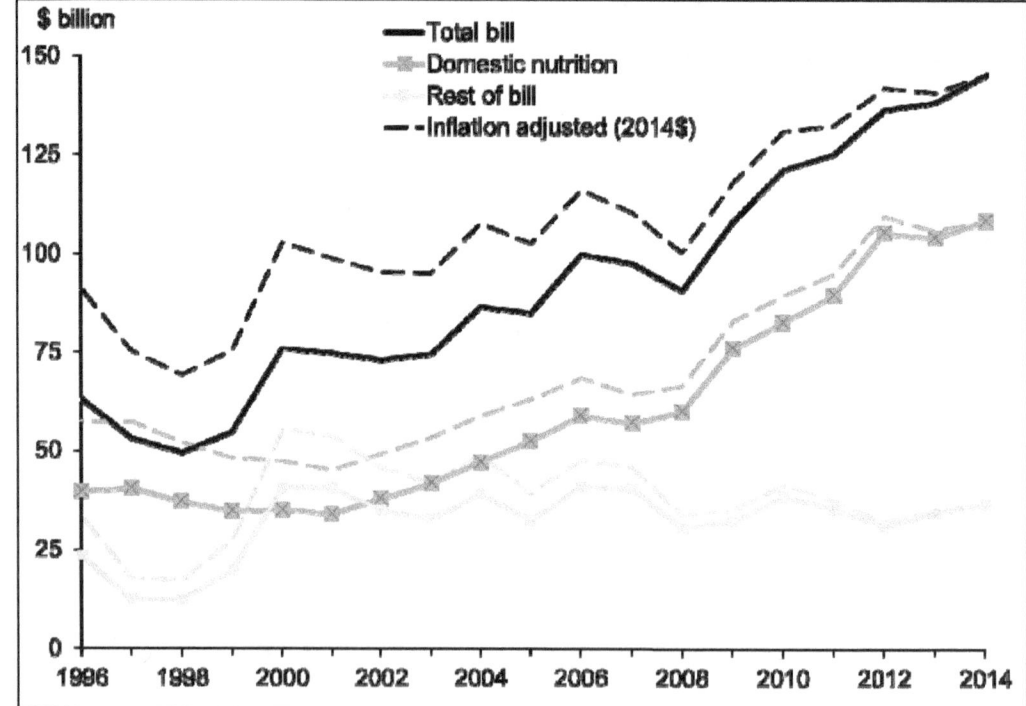

Source: CRS. Fiscal year budget authority. Inflation-adjusted amounts are based on the GDP price deflator.

Notes: The largest domestic nutrition programs are the child nutrition programs, SNAP, and WIC. The "rest of bill" includes USDA (except the Forest Service), FDA and CFTC.

Within the discretionary subtotal of **Figure A-1**, a similar domestic nutrition vs. rest of the bill comparison can be made as was done for the total appropriation (see **Figure A-3**).

- As stated before, total discretionary Agriculture appropriations grew at +2.2% per year over the past 10 years, and were nearly constant on an inflation-adjusted level. This component of the appropriation is arguably where appropriators have the most control.

  Over the five-year period since FY2009, the annual change is +0.3% per year, or -1.5% per year on an inflation-adjusted basis.

- The domestic nutrition portion of this discretionary subtotal (primarily WIC, commodity assistance programs, and nutrition programs administration) shows a +3.9% average annual increase over 10 years (+1.6% per year on an inflation-adjusted basis).

  Over the five-year period, the annual change is -0.2% per year, or -2.0% per year on an inflation-adjusted basis.

- The discretionary portion for rest of the bill has an average annual 10-year increase +1.4% (-0.8% per year on an inflation-adjusted basis).

  Over the five-year period, the annual change is +0.5% per year, or -1.2% per year on an inflation-adjusted basis.

Figure A-3. Discretionary Agriculture Appropriations

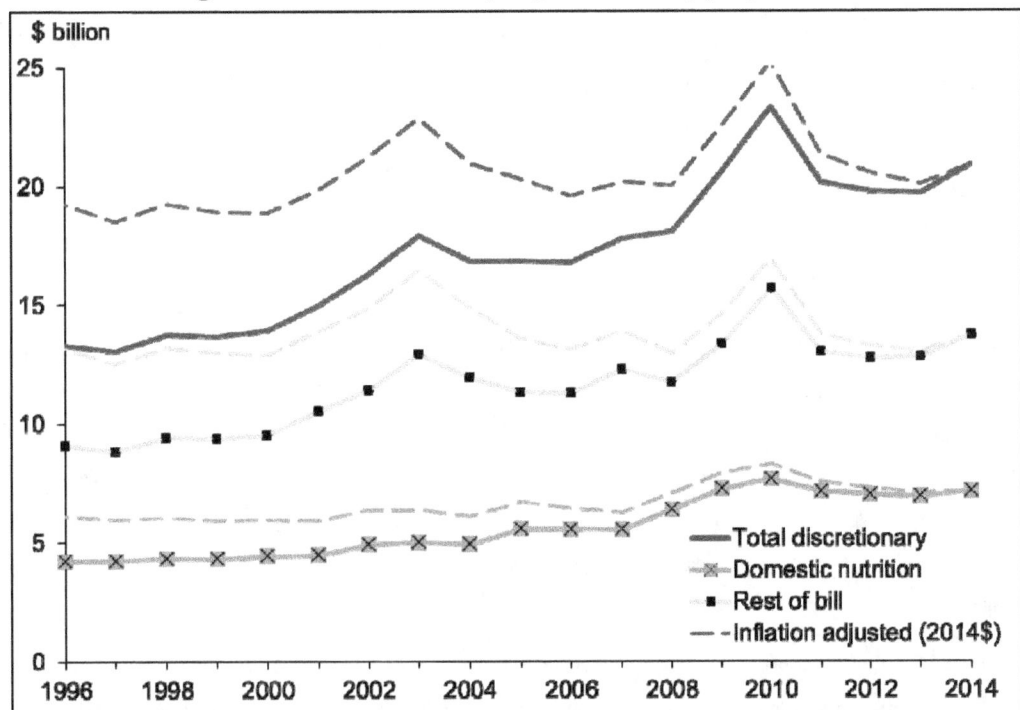

Source: CRS. Fiscal year budget authority. Inflation-adjusted amounts are based on the GDP price deflator.
Notes: Includes only regular annual appropriations for USDA (except the Forest Service), FDA, and CFTC (regardless of jurisdiction). The label "Domestic nutrition" includes WIC, commodity assistance programs, and nutrition programs administration.

Table A-1. Trends in Nominal Agriculture Appropriations

(fiscal year budget authority in billions of dollars, except as noted)

	1995	1996	1997	1998	1999	2000	2001	2002	2003	2004
Discretionary total	13.29	13.31	13.04	13.75	13.69	13.95	14.97	16.28	17.91	16.84
Domestic nutrition	3.93	4.22	4.22	4.31	4.31	4.42	4.46	4.89	5.00	4.90
Rest of bill	9.36	9.09	8.82	9.44	9.39	9.53	10.51	11.39	12.91	11.94
Mandatory total	54.61	49.78	40.08	35.80	41.00	61.95	59.77	56.91	56.70	69.75
Domestic nutrition	36.30	35.54	36.27	32.91	30.51	30.63	29.66	33.06	36.89	42.36
Rest of bill	18.31	14.23	3.81	2.89	10.48	31.33	30.12	23.86	19.82	27.38
Total bill	67.90	63.09	53.12	49.55	54.69	75.90	74.74	73.19	74.61	86.59
Domestic nutrition	40.23	39.76	40.49	37.22	34.82	35.04	34.12	37.95	41.89	47.26
Rest of bill	27.67	23.33	12.63	12.33	19.87	40.85	40.63	35.24	32.72	39.32
Percentages of Total										
1. Mandatory	80%	79%	75%	72%	75%	82%	80%	78%	76%	81%
2. Discretionary	20%	21%	25%	28%	25%	18%	20%	22%	24%	19%
1. Domestic nutrition	59%	63%	76%	75%	64%	46%	46%	52%	56%	55%
2. Rest of bill	41%	37%	24%	25%	36%	54%	54%	48%	44%	45%

	2005	2006	2007	2008	2009	2010	2011	2012	2013	2014
Discretionary total	16.83	16.78	17.81	18.09	20.60	23.30	20.13	19.76	19.72	20.88
Domestic nutrition	5.55	5.53	5.52	6.37	7.23	7.65	7.13	7.00	6.93	7.15
Rest of bill	11.28	11.25	12.29	11.72	13.37	15.65	13.00	12.76	12.79	13.73
Mandatory total	68.29	83.07	79.80	72.67	87.80	97.98	105.13	116.85	118.75	124.58
Domestic nutrition	46.94	53.37	51.51	53.68	68.92	75.13	82.53	98.55	97.17	101.43
Rest of bill	21.36	29.70	28.29	18.99	18.88	22.86	22.60	18.29	21.58	23.15
Total bill	85.13	99.85	97.61	90.76	108.40	121.29	125.26	136.61	138.47	145.46
Domestic nutrition	52.49	58.89	57.03	60.06	76.16	82.78	89.66	105.55	104.10	108.59
Rest of bill	32.64	40.95	40.58	30.71	32.24	38.50	35.61	31.05	34.37	36.88
Percentages of Total										
1. Mandatory	80%	83%	82%	80%	81%	81%	84%	86%	86%	86%
2. Discretionary	20%	17%	18%	20%	19%	19%	16%	14%	14%	14%
1. Domestic nutrition	62%	59%	58%	66%	70%	68%	72%	77%	75%	75%
2. Rest of bill	38%	41%	42%	34%	30%	32%	28%	23%	25%	25%

Source: CRS. Regular appropriations only; all years include Commodity Futures Trading Commission.

a. The largest domestic nutrition programs are the child nutrition programs, the Supplemental Nutrition Assistance Program (SNAP, formerly food stamps)—both of which are mandatory—and the Special Supplemental Nutrition Program for Women, Infants, and Children (WIC), which is discretionary.

b. "Rest of bill" includes the non-nutrition remainder of USDA (except the Forest Service), FDA, and CFTC. Within that group, mandatory programs include the farm commodity programs, crop insurance, and some conservation and foreign aid/trade programs.

Table A-2. Trends in Real Agriculture Appropriations

(fiscal year budget authority in billions of dollars, except as noted)

	1995	1996	1997	1998	1999	2000	2001	2002	2003	2004
GDP price index[a]	81.84	83.42	84.95	86.03	87.17	88.97	91.06	92.57	94.46	96.85
Inflation-adjusted 2014 dollars (real dollars)										
Discretionary total	**19.58**	**19.23**	**18.51**	**19.27**	**18.93**	**18.89**	**19.82**	**21.19**	**22.85**	**20.96**
Domestic nutrition	5.79	6.10	5.99	6.04	5.95	5.99	5.90	6.37	6.38	6.10
Rest of bill	13.79	13.14	12.52	13.22	12.98	12.91	13.91	14.83	16.47	14.86
Mandatory total	**80.43**	**71.93**	**56.87**	**50.16**	**56.69**	**83.94**	**79.12**	**74.11**	**72.36**	**86.81**
Domestic nutrition	53.47	51.36	51.47	46.11	42.19	41.49	39.26	43.04	47.07	52.73
Rest of bill	26.97	20.57	5.40	4.05	14.50	42.44	39.86	31.06	25.29	34.08
Total bill	**100.01**	**91.16**	**75.37**	**69.43**	**75.62**	**102.83**	**98.94**	**95.30**	**95.21**	**107.76**
Domestic nutrition	59.25	57.46	57.45	52.15	48.15	47.48	45.16	49.41	53.46	58.82
Rest of bill	40.76	33.70	17.92	17.27	27.48	55.35	53.78	45.89	41.76	48.94
	2005	**2006**	**2007**	**2008**	**2009**	**2010**	**2011**	**2012**	**2013**	**2014**
GDP price index[a]	100.00	103.40	106.46	108.93	110.33	111.45	113.79	115.88	118.30	120.54
Inflation-adjusted 2014 dollars (real dollars)										
Discretionary total	**20.29**	**19.56**	**20.17**	**20.02**	**22.51**	**25.20**	**21.33**	**20.56**	**20.09**	**20.88**
Domestic nutrition	6.69	6.44	6.25	7.05	7.90	8.28	7.55	7.28	7.06	7.15
Rest of bill	13.60	13.12	13.91	12.97	14.60	16.93	13.78	13.27	13.03	13.73
Mandatory total	**82.32**	**96.84**	**90.35**	**80.42**	**95.92**	**105.98**	**111.37**	**121.54**	**121.00**	**124.58**
Domestic nutrition	56.58	62.21	58.32	59.40	75.30	81.26	87.42	102.52	99.01	101.43
Rest of bill	25.74	34.62	32.04	21.01	20.62	24.72	23.95	19.03	21.99	23.15
Total bill	**102.61**	**116.40**	**110.52**	**100.44**	**118.43**	**131.18**	**132.70**	**142.10**	**141.09**	**145.46**
Domestic nutrition	63.27	68.66	64.57	66.46	83.20	89.53	94.97	109.80	106.07	108.59
Rest of bill	39.34	47.74	45.95	33.98	35.23	41.65	37.72	32.30	35.02	36.88

Source: CRS. Regular appropriations only; all years include Commodity Futures Trading Commission. See footnotes in **Table A-1** for definitions of "domestic nutrition" and "rest of bill."

a. OMB, Budget of the United States Government, "Historical Tables," Table 10.1, at http://www.whitehouse.gov/omb/budget/Historicals.

Table A-3. Percentage Changes in Agriculture Appropriations

	Average annual (compounded) rate of change from years in the past to FY2014							
	Actual Change (Nominal)				Inflation-Adjusted (Real) Change (2014 $)			
	FY2013 (1 yr.)	FY2009 (5 yrs.)	FY2004 (10 yrs.)	FY1999 (15 yrs.)	FY2013 (1 yr.)	FY2009 (5 yrs.)	FY2004 (10 yrs.)	FY1999 (15 yrs.)
Discretionary total	+5.9%	+0.3%	+2.2%	+2.9%	+3.9%	-1.5%	-0.0%	+0.7%
Domestic nutrition	+3.3%	-0.2%	+3.9%	+3.4%	+1.4%	-2.0%	+1.6%	+1.2%
Rest of bill	+7.3%	+0.5%	+1.4%	+2.6%	+5.3%	-1.2%	-0.8%	+0.4%
Mandatory total	+4.9%	+7.2%	+6.0%	+7.7%	+3.0%	+5.4%	+3.7%	+5.4%
Domestic nutrition	+4.4%	+8.0%	+9.1%	+8.3%	+2.4%	+6.1%	+6.8%	+6.0%
Rest of bill	+7.3%	+4.2%	-1.7%	+5.4%	+5.3%	+2.3%	-3.8%	+3.2%
Total bill	+5.0%	+6.1%	+5.3%	+6.7%	+3.1%	+4.2%	+3.0%	+4.5%
Domestic nutrition	+4.3%	+7.4%	+8.7%	+7.9%	+2.4%	+5.5%	+6.3%	+5.6%
Rest of bill	+7.3%	+2.7%	-0.6%	+4.2%	+5.3%	+0.9%	-2.8%	+2.0%

Source: CRS calculations of the compounded annual rate of change between FY2014 and the stated prior year. Regular appropriations only; all years include Commodity Futures Trading Commission. See footnotes in **Table A-1** for definitions of "domestic nutrition" and "rest of bill."

Comparisons to the Federal Budget, GDP, and Population

Relative to the entire federal budget, the Agriculture bill's share has declined from over 4% of the total federal budget in FY1995 and FY2000 to 2.7% in FY2009, before rising again to nearly that level since the recession, to 3.8% in FY2014 (**Figure A-4**, **Table A-4**). Within that total, the share for nutrition programs had declined from 2.6% in FY1995 to 1.8% in FY2008, but the recent recession has caused that share to rise to about 2.9% in FY2014. The share for the rest of the bill has declined from 2.1% in FY2001 to about 1.0% in FY2014.

Those shares of the federal budget also can be subdivided into mandatory and discretionary spending (**Figure A-5**). The mandatory share for nutrition is presently about 2.7% (generally rising, but recently ameliorating), while the discretionary share for nutrition is fairly steady 0.2%. The mandatory share for the rest of the bill (primarily crop insurance, commodity program subsidies, and conservation) is about 0.6%, while the discretionary share for the rest of the bill is about 0.4% (generally declining).

The 0.6% share of the federal budget above for mandatory spending on crop insurance, farm commodity subsidies, and conservation is a good proxy for farm bill spending on agricultural (non-nutrition) programs (**Figure A-5**). It has been variable and generally declining since 2000 (consistent with farm commodity spending), though since 2009 steadier to slightly rising (consistent with steady to declining farm commodity spending but increasing crop insurance and mandatory conservation spending).

Figure A-4. Agriculture Appropriations as Percentages of Total Federal Budget

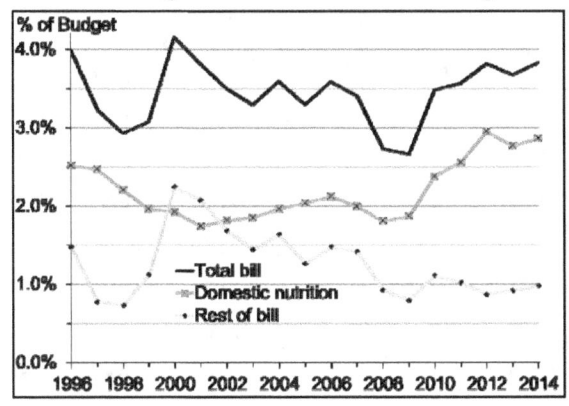

Source: CRS.

Figure A-5. More Components as Percentages of Total Federal Budget

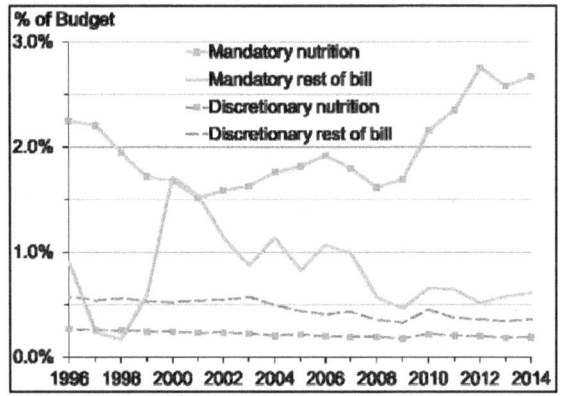

Source: CRS.

As a percentage of gross domestic product (GDP),[135] Agriculture appropriations had been fairly steady at under 0.75% of GDP from FY2000-FY2009, but have risen to about 0.86% of GDP in FY2014 (**Figure A-6**, **Table A-4**) due to increases in nutrition program demand. Nutrition programs have been rising as a percentage of GDP since FY2000 (0.33% in FY2001 to 0.64% in FY2014), while non-nutrition agricultural programs have declined (0.42% in FY2000 to 0.22% in FY2014).

On a per capita basis, inflation-adjusted total Agriculture appropriations have risen slightly over the past 10 to 15 years from about $250 per capita in 1998 (FY2014 dollars) to about $450 per capita in FY2014 (**Figure A-7**). Nutrition programs have risen more steadily on a per capita basis from about $160 per capita in FY2001 to nearly $350 per capita in FY2014. Non-nutrition "other" agricultural programs have been more steady or declining, falling from nearly $200 per capita in 2000 to about $115 per capita in FY2014.

Figure A-6. Agriculture Appropriations as Percentages of GDP

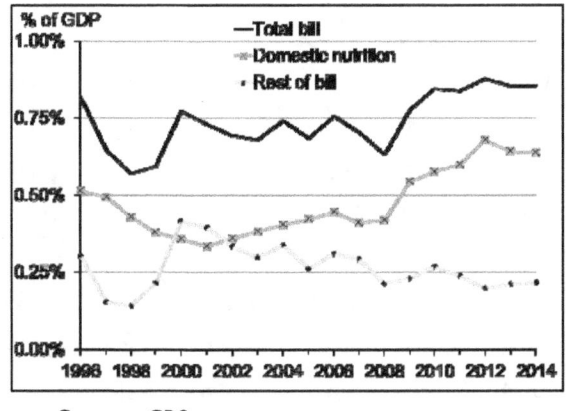

Source: CRS.

Figure A-7. Agriculture Appropriations per Capita of U.S. Population

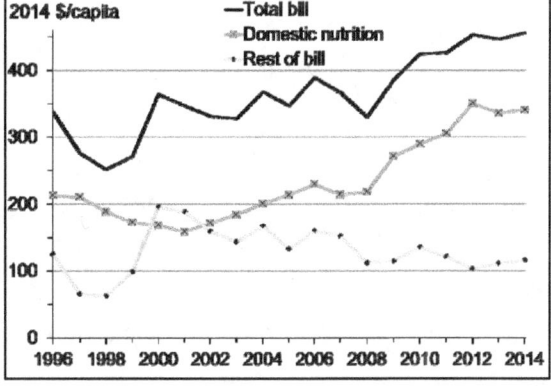

Source: CRS.

---

[135] Two other CRS reports compare various components of federal spending against GDP at a more aggregate level. See CRS Report RL33074, *Mandatory Spending Since 1962*, and CRS Report RL34424, *The Budget Control Act and Trends in Discretionary Spending*.

Table A-4. Trends in Agriculture Appropriations Measured Against Benchmarks

(fiscal year)

	1995	1996	1997	1998	1999	2000	2001	2002	2003	2004
Federal Budget ($ billions)	1,540	1,581	1,643	1,692	1,777	1,825	1,959	2,090	2,266	2,408
GDP ($ billions)	7,341	7,718	8,212	8,663	9,208	9,821	10,225	10,544	10,980	11,676
Population (million)	266.6	269.7	272.9	276.1	279.3	282.4	285.3	288.0	290.7	293.3
Pct. of Federal Budget	**4.41%**	**3.99%**	**3.23%**	**2.93%**	**3.08%**	**4.16%**	**3.82%**	**3.50%**	**3.29%**	**3.60%**
Domestic nutrition	2.61%	2.52%	2.46%	2.20%	1.96%	1.92%	1.74%	1.82%	1.85%	1.96%
Mandatory	*2.36%*	*2.25%*	*2.21%*	*1.94%*	*1.72%*	*1.68%*	*1.51%*	*1.58%*	*1.63%*	*1.76%*
Discretionary	*0.26%*	*0.27%*	*0.26%*	*0.25%*	*0.24%*	*0.24%*	*0.23%*	*0.23%*	*0.22%*	*0.20%*
Rest of bill	1.80%	1.48%	0.77%	0.73%	1.12%	2.24%	2.07%	1.69%	1.44%	1.63%
Mandatory	*1.19%*	*0.90%*	*0.23%*	*0.17%*	*0.59%*	*1.72%*	*1.54%*	*1.14%*	*0.87%*	*1.14%*
Discretionary	*0.61%*	*0.58%*	*0.54%*	*0.56%*	*0.53%*	*0.52%*	*0.54%*	*0.54%*	*0.57%*	*0.50%*
Pct. of GDP	**0.92%**	**0.82%**	**0.65%**	**0.57%**	**0.59%**	**0.77%**	**0.73%**	**0.69%**	**0.68%**	**0.74%**
Domestic nutrition	0.55%	0.52%	0.49%	0.43%	0.38%	0.36%	0.33%	0.36%	0.38%	0.40%
Rest of bill	0.38%	0.30%	0.15%	0.14%	0.22%	0.42%	0.40%	0.33%	0.30%	0.34%
Per capita (2014 dollars)	**375**	**338**	**276**	**251**	**271**	**364**	**347**	**331**	**328**	**367**
Domestic nutrition	222	213	211	189	172	168	158	172	184	201
Rest of bill	153	125	66	63	98	196	189	159	144	167

	2005	2006	2007	2008	2009	2010	2011	2012	2013	2014
U.S. budget authority ($ billions)	2,583	2,780	2,863	3,326	4,077	3,485	3,510	3,576	3,767	3,796
GDP ($ billions)	12,429	13,207	13,861	14,334	13,961	14,348	14,929	15,547	16,203	17,011
Population (million)	296.0	298.8	301.7	304.5	307.2	309.3	311.6	313.9	316.1	318.9
Pct. of Federal Budget	**3.30%**	**3.59%**	**3.41%**	**2.73%**	**2.66%**	**3.48%**	**3.57%**	**3.82%**	**3.68%**	**3.83%**
Domestic nutrition	2.03%	2.12%	1.99%	1.81%	1.87%	2.38%	2.55%	2.95%	2.76%	2.86%
Mandatory	*1.82%*	*1.92%*	*1.80%*	*1.61%*	*1.69%*	*2.16%*	*2.35%*	*2.76%*	*2.58%*	*2.67%*
Discretionary	*0.21%*	*0.20%*	*0.19%*	*0.19%*	*0.18%*	*0.22%*	*0.20%*	*0.20%*	*0.18%*	*0.19%*
Rest of bill	1.26%	1.47%	1.42%	0.92%	0.79%	1.10%	1.01%	0.87%	0.91%	0.97%
Mandatory	*0.83%*	*1.07%*	*0.99%*	*0.57%*	*0.46%*	*0.66%*	*0.64%*	*0.51%*	*0.57%*	*0.61%*
Discretionary	*0.44%*	*0.40%*	*0.43%*	*0.35%*	*0.33%*	*0.45%*	*0.37%*	*0.36%*	*0.34%*	*0.36%*
Pct. of GDP	**0.68%**	**0.76%**	**0.70%**	**0.63%**	**0.78%**	**0.85%**	**0.84%**	**0.88%**	**0.85%**	**0.86%**
Domestic nutrition	0.42%	0.45%	0.41%	0.42%	0.55%	0.58%	0.60%	0.68%	0.64%	0.64%
Rest of bill	0.26%	0.31%	0.29%	0.21%	0.23%	0.27%	0.24%	0.20%	0.21%	0.22%
Per capita (2014 dollars)	**347**	**390**	**366**	**330**	**386**	**424**	**426**	**453**	**446**	**456**
Domestic nutrition	214	230	214	218	271	289	305	350	336	341
Rest of bill	133	160	152	112	115	135	121	103	111	116

Source: CRS. Federal budget and GDP from OMB, Budget of the United States, "Historical Tables," Table 5.1 (total budget authority), and Table 10.1, respectively. Populations from Census Bureau Population Projections, and *Statistical Abstract of the United States*. See **Table A-1** for definitions of "domestic nutrition" and "rest of bill."

Author Contact Information

Jim Monke, Coordinator
Specialist in Agricultural Policy
jmonke@crs.loc.gov, 7-9664

Randy Alison Aussenberg
Analyst in Nutrition Assistance Policy
raussenberg@crs.loc.gov, 7-8641

Megan Stubbs
Specialist in Agricultural Conservation and Natural
Resources Policy
mstubbs@crs.loc.gov, 7-8707

Renée Johnson
Specialist in Agricultural Policy
rjohnson@crs.loc.gov, 7-9588

Joel L. Greene
Analyst in Agricultural Policy
jgreene@crs.loc.gov, 7-9877

Susan Thaul
Specialist in Drug Safety and Effectiveness
sthaul@crs.loc.gov, 7-0562

Tadlock Cowan
Analyst in Natural Resources and Rural
Development
tcowan@crs.loc.gov, 7-7600

Dennis A. Shields
Specialist in Agricultural Policy
dshields@crs.loc.gov, 7-9051

Randy Schnepf
Specialist in Agricultural Policy
rschnepf@crs.loc.gov, 7-4277

Remy Jurenas
Specialist in Agricultural Policy
rjurenas@crs.loc.gov, 7-7281

Rena S. Miller
Specialist in Financial Economics
rsmiller@crs.loc.gov, 7-0826